OLD TESTAMENT
PROPHETS

A Supplement to the Preacher's Outline & Sermon Bible

_____

_____

LEADERSHIP
MINISTRIES WORLDWIDE

COPYRIGHT © 2014
By Alpha-Omega Ministries, Inc.
All rights reserved. No part of *The Preacher's
Outline & Sermon Bible®*, including its outlines,
study helps, or indexes, may be reproduced in any
manner without written permission.

The Preacher's Outline & Sermon Bible® is written for God's people to use in their preparation for preaching and teaching. Leadership Ministries Worldwide wants God's people to use *The Preacher's Outline & Sermon Bible®*. The purpose of the copyright is to prevent the reproduction, misuse, and abuse of the material.

May our Lord bless us all as we preach, teach, and write for Him, fulfilling His great commission to make disciples of all nations.

Please address all requests for information or permission to:
    Leadership Ministries Worldwide
    1928 Central Avenue
    Chattanooga, TN 37408
    Ph.# (423) 855-2181   FAX (423) 855-8616   E-Mail info@lmw.org
    http://www.lmw.org

Library of Congress Catalog Card Number: 00-133499
International Standard Book Number: 978-1-57407-295-2

Printed in the United States of America

1   2   3   4   5   14   15   16   17   18

LEADERSHIP MINISTRIES WORLDWIDE

DEDICATED

To all the men and women of the world
who preach and teach the Gospel of
our Lord Jesus Christ and
to the Mercy and Grace of God

&

- Demonstrated to us in Christ Jesus our Lord.

  In him we have redemption through his blood, the forgiveness of sins, in accordance with the riches of God's grace. (Ep.1:7)

- Out of the mercy and grace of God, His Word has flowed. Let every person know that God will have mercy upon him, forgiving and using him to fulfill His glorious plan of salvation.

  For God so loved the world that he gave his one and only Son, that whoever believes in him shall not perish but have eternal life. For God did not send his Son into the world to condemn the world, but to save the world through him. (Jn.3:16-17)

  This is good, and pleases God our Savior, who wants all men to be saved and to come to a knowledge of the truth. (1 Ti.2:3-4)

6/10

The Preacher's Outline & Sermon Bible®

is written for God's servants to use in their study, teaching, and preaching of God's Holy Word...

- to share the Word of God with the world.
- to help believers, both ministers and laypersons, in their understanding, preaching, and teaching of God's Word.
- to do everything we possibly can to lead men, women, boys, and girls to give their hearts and lives to Jesus Christ and to secure the eternal life that He offers.
- to do all we can to minister to the needy of the world.
- to give Jesus Christ His proper place, the place the Word gives Him. Therefore, no work of Leadership Ministries Worldwide—no Outline Bible Resources—will ever be personalized.

*Woe to me if I do not
preach the gospel!*
(1 Co.9:16)

THE PROPHETS: THEIR MESSAGE—THEN AND NOW

Dear Friends,

This booklet is a vital resource and companion to *The Preacher's Outline & Sermon Bible* volumes on *Isaiah* through *Malachi*. In it you will find a wealth of information to enhance your preparation of meaningful lessons and/or messages from any of these great books of the Bible.

The prophets were called and chosen by God to do two things:
- ➤ to proclaim God's salvation to the world
- ➤ to prophesy and predict how God was going to save humanity

Both functions were necessary. The prophet had to proclaim salvation to the people of his own generation and to predict how God was going to save the people of all generations. But note: the predictions of the future salvation were not the prophet's own predictions. He had not been called to proclaim his own ideas or message; he had been called to proclaim the salvation of God Himself. He was a man given a very special call, a call to the most important task in all the world: the task of proclaiming the glory and wonder of God's salvation. God was making it possible for man to be saved and to live eternally.

The prophet conveyed the salvation of God...
- by pointing out the sins of the people
- by warning the people about the terrible and certain consequences of sin, the discipline and judgment of God
- by encouraging the people to repent by wholeheartedly turning back to God, worshipping Him and Him alone
- by proclaiming God's eternal plan of salvation and blessings to those who would believe

Speaking of the prophets, Peter Adams writes, "To respond to God's words is to respond to God."[1]

But this is how God fulfilled what he had foretold through all the prophets, saying that his Christ would suffer. Repent, then, and turn to God, so that your sins may be wiped out, that times of refreshing may come from the Lord, and that he may send the Christ, who has been appointed for you—even Jesus. He must remain in heaven until the time comes for God to restore everything, as he promised long ago through his holy prophets. For Moses said, 'The Lord your God will raise up for you a prophet like me from among your own people; you must listen to everything he tells you. Anyone who does not listen to him will be completely cut off from among his people.' "Indeed, all the prophets from Samuel on, as many as have spoken, have foretold these days. And you are heirs of the prophets and of the covenant God made with your fathers. He said to Abraham, 'Through your offspring all peoples on earth will be blessed.' When God raised up his servant, he sent him first to you to bless you by turning each of you from your wicked ways" (Ac.3:18-26).

The Books of the Bible written by the prophets of God contain as many valuable lessons for us today as they did for those to whom the prophets originally spoke. It is our prayer that this booklet will enrich your study and message and help all who sit under your preaching or teaching to grow more faithful to the Lord day by day.

Your fellow servants at...

LEADERSHIP MINISTRIES WORLDWIDE

---

1 Peter Adams. *Speaking God's Words.* (Downers Grove, IL: Inter-Varsity Press, 1996), pp.19-20.

THE PROPHETS

ALPHABETICAL LISTING OF THE PROPHETS

NAME	DATE
Abel	Right after creation
Abraham	2000 B.C.
Agabus	A.D. 43
Ahijah	931–910 B.C.
Amos	750 B.C.
Anna	4 B.C.
Asaph	1004 B.C.
Azariah	896 B.C.
Daniel	605–535 B.C.
David	1029–971 B.C.
Deborah	1220 B.C.
Eliezer	849–848 B.C.
Elijah	860–845 B.C.
Elisha	850–795 B.C.
Ezekiel	593–571 B.C.
Gad	1015–950 B.C.
Habakkuk	615–598 B.C.
Haggai	520 B.C.
Hanani	870 B.C.
Heman	971 B.C.
Hosea	788–723 B.C.
Huldah	623 B.C.
Iddo	910 B.C.
Isaiah	740–690 B.C.
Jacob/Israel	1858 B.C.
Jehu	886 B.C.
Jeremiah	627–562 B.C.
Joel	830 B.C.
John the Apostle	A.D. 95
John the Baptist	A.D. 26
Jonah	780–765 B.C.
Joseph	1900–1885 B.C.
Malachi	430 B.C.
Micah	735–725 B.C.
Micaiah	853 B.C.
Moses	1405 B.C.

NAME	DATE
Nahum	663–612 B.C.
Nathan	1003–931 B.C.
Noah	At least seven generations after Adam
Obadiah	845 B.C.
Oded	733 B.C.
Paul	A.D. 35–64
Shemaiah	926 B.C.
Unnamed prophet Prophesied a total victory over the Syrians	855 B.C.
Unnamed prophet Prophesied a victory over the Syrians	856 B.C.
Unnamed prophet Rebuked Eli and his house for profaning the temple	1085 B.C.
Unnamed prophet Rebuked Israel for fearing idols	1210 B.C.
Unnamed prophet Rebuked King Ahab for sparing the evil Ben-Hadad	855 B.C.
Unnamed prophet Rebuked King Amaziah for his idolatry	767 B.C.
Unnamed prophet Rebuked King Jeroboam I for his idolatry	931 B.C.
Unnamed prophet Warned King Amaziah not to hire Israel's army	767 B.C.
Urijah	608 B.C.
Zechariah, son of Jehoiada	797 B.C.
Zephaniah	640–609 B.C.

THE PROPHETS

CHRONOLOGICAL LISTING OF THE PROPHETS[2]

NAME	DATE
Abel	Right after creation
Noah	At least seven generations after Adam
Abraham	2000 B.C.
Joseph	1900–1885 B.C.
Jacob/Israel	1858 B.C.
Moses	1405 B.C.
Deborah	1220 B.C.
Unnamed prophet Rebuked Israel for fearing idols	1210 B.C.
Samuel	1095–1015 B.C.
Unnamed prophet Rebuked Eli and his house for profaning the temple	1085 B.C.
David	1029–971 B.C.
Gad	1015–950 B.C.
Asaph	1004 B.C.
Nathan	1003-931 B.C.
Heman	971 B.C.
Unnamed prophet Rebuked King Jeroboam I for his idolatry	931 B.C.
Ahijah	931–910 B.C.
Shemaiah	926 B.C.
Iddo	910 B.C.
Azariah	896 B.C.
Jehu	886 B.C.
Hanani	870 B.C.
Elijah	860–845 B.C.
Unnamed prophet Prophesied a victory over the Syrians	856 B.C.
Unnamed prophet Prophesied total victory over the Syrians	855 B.C.
Unnamed prophet Rebuked King Ahab for sparing the evil Ben-Hadad	855 B.C.

NAME	DATE
Micaiah	853 B.C.
Elisha	850–795 B.C.
Eliezer	849–848 B.C.
Obadiah	845 B.C.
Joel	830 B.C.
Zechariah, son of Jehoiada	797 B.C.
Hosea	788–723 B.C.
Jonah	780–765 B.C.
Unnamed prophet Rebuked King Amaziah for his idolatry	767 B.C.
Unnamed prophet Warned King Amaziah not to hire Israel's army	767 B.C.
Amos	750 B.C.
Isaiah	740–690 B.C.
Micah	735–725 B.C.
Oded	733 B.C.
Nahum	663–612 B.C.
Zephaniah	640–609 B.C.
Jeremiah	627–562 B.C.
Huldah	623 B.C.
Habakkuk	615–598 B.C.
Urijah	608 B.C.
Daniel	605–535 B.C.
Ezekiel	593–571 B.C.
Haggai	520 B.C.
Zechariah, son of Berechiah	520–518 B.C.
Malachi	430 B.C.
Anna	4 B.C.
John the Baptist	A.D. 26
Paul	A.D. 35–64
Agabus	A.D. 43
John the Apostle	A.D. 95

---

2 The list above serves as a timeline for all the prophets discussed in the following chart. The unnamed prophets are listed according to their message. (Also see the *Timeline of Kings, Prophets, and History* chart, pp.72-73.)

THE PROPHETS

PROPHET	TIME/PLACE GIVEN	MAIN MESSAGE	PRACTICAL APPLICATION
ABEL (Breath) **Known Facts** 1. Was the son of Adam (Ge.4:2). 2. Was called a prophet by Jesus Christ (Mt. 23:34-35; Lu. 11:50-51). 3. Kept the flocks of animals (Ge.4:2). 4. Brought an acceptable and pleasing sacrifice to God (Ge. 4:4). 5. Was murdered by his brother, Cain (Ge.4:8). 6. Was avenged by God (Ge.4:9-12). **Predictions and Messages** By example he taught that a person must approach God through the sacrifice of a substitute offering (Ge.4:4). **Scripture References** Ge.4:1-16; Mt.23:34-39; Lu.11:47-51; He.11:4; 12:24	**Time** *The first years after creation, when Adam was still alive.* **Place** *Outside the garden of Eden, where man first began to farm.*	Abel's message is seen in his worship. Note what Abel did: when he approached the LORD, he brought an animal, a blood sacrifice. Why? Because his father, Adam, had taught him to approach God through the sacrifice of an animal. God taught Adam… • that sin causes death • that an innocent substitute had to sacrificially die in order to clothe man's shame and guilt • that thereafter man could only approach God through the sacrificial death of an innocent substitute Thus Abel pointed forward to Christ, the perfect sacrifice. He may not have completely understood, but Abel did approach God through the blood sacrifice, just as his father had taught him. Abel had *faith*. He believed that God would forgive his sins and accept him through the sacrifice of an innocent life. And note the remarkable testimony Scripture gives about Abel's faith in the coming Savior: Abel even today, although dead, testifies of Christ (He.11:4). What a striking legacy Abel left to the world! **But Abel brought fat portions from some of the firstborn of his flock. The LORD looked with favor on Abel and his offering (Ge.4:4).** **By faith Abel offered God a better sacrifice than Cain did. By faith he was commended as a righteous man, when God spoke well of his offerings. And by faith he still speaks, even though he is dead (He.11:4).** **To Jesus the mediator of a new covenant, and to the sprinkled blood that speaks a better word than the blood of Abel (He.12:24).**	No person can earn, win, or merit salvation. No person can approach God through his own works, energy, efforts, fruits, ways, religion, ceremony or ritual. The reason is clearly evident: no person is perfect. We have a sin problem and a death problem that has to be taken care of before we can ever become acceptable to God. God has taken care of this in the sacrifice of His Son for our sins. Jesus Christ took our sins upon Himself and died for them. This is what the sacrifice of the innocent life symbolized in the Old Testament. Just like Abel, we must believe God, believe that the death (the blood) of the sacrifice of Jesus Christ covers our sins. God accepts no person apart from Jesus Christ, the promised seed and Savior of the world. God has never accepted *any person* apart from the shedding of the blood of His dear Son. The blood of Christ had to be shed for all persons through all the generations of human history. Apart from Christ, apart from accepting His sacrifice, no person can be saved from sin. No person can escape the judgment of death and hell apart from Christ. **"You snakes! You brood of vipers! How will you escape being condemned to hell? (Mt.23:33).** **You see, at just the right time, when we were still powerless, Christ died for the ungodly (Ro.5:6).** **For what I received I passed on to you as of first importance: that Christ died for our sins according to the Scriptures (1 Co.15:3).** **And live a life of love, just as Christ loved us and gave himself up for us as a fragrant offering and sacrifice to God (Ep.5:2).**

PROPHET	TIME/PLACE GIVEN	MAIN MESSAGE	PRACTICAL APPLICATION
AGABUS (Locust) **Known Facts** 1. Lived in Judea near Jerusalem (Ac.21:10). 2. Ministered among a company of prophets (Ac.11:27-28). 3. Prophesied with the words of the Holy Spirit (Ac.11:28; 21:11). 4. Spoke for the prophets (Ac.11:28). **Predictions and Messages** 1. A severe famine would come to the entire Roman world (Ac.11:28). 2. The Apostle Paul would be bound and taken prisoner, and eventually killed (Ac. 21:11-13). **Scripture References** Ac.11:27-30; 21:10-14	**Time** *A.D. 43, at the beginning of the terrible persecution of Agrippa.* **Place** *Antioch of Syria, where the followers of Jesus Christ were first called Christians.*	Agabus prophesied two future events by the Spirit of God. First, Agabus prophesied that a great famine would occur. The disciples accepted the message given and gathered funds and stores of food to be used for those in need. Note this fact: the disciples did not waste time questioning God; they simply acted immediately on the information given, doing what was necessary for the church to continue. Some time later, Agabus prophesied that the Gentiles (or Romans) would take the Apostle Paul prisoner. Despite the danger of suffering and persecution, and eventually death, Paul was unhindered in his mission to preach the gospel. Knowing the prophecy, the fire of devotion within Paul burned all the more. Why? Because Paul trusted God. He understood that nothing is out of God's control. He firmly believed that as long as he continued to do the will of the Lord, the Lord would richly bless his labor for the gospel. **During this time some prophets came down from Jerusalem to Antioch. One of them, named Agabus, stood up and through the Spirit predicted that a severe famine would spread over the entire Roman world. (This happened during the reign of Claudius.) (Ac.11:27-28).** **After we had been there a number of days, a prophet named Agabus came down from Judea. Coming over to us, he took Paul's belt, tied his own hands and feet with it and said, "The Holy Spirit says, 'In this way the Jews of Jerusalem will bind the owner of this belt and will hand him over to the Gentiles'" (Ac.21:10-11).**	1. Giving is essential. Believers must give to those in need. And they should practice regular giving, not waiting for some disaster to strike and then scrambling for a solution to the problem. Giving should be a regular habit of the believer so the mission of the church can be carried out, even in difficult times. 2. Believers will suffer. Believers suffer by: ➢ being ridiculed ➢ being mocked ➢ being assaulted ➢ being spoken evil of ➢ being gossiped about ➢ being slandered ➢ being reviled ➢ being insulted ➢ being scolded ➢ being falsely accused ➢ being put on trial ➢ even being murdered But suffering is necessary. First of all, believers must live out the calling given to them by the Lord no matter how unpleasant, no matter what the cost. Second, suffering prepares the believer to participate in the glory of Christ. It is the necessary condition for exaltation. Suffering and struggling are a refining process through which the believer must pass. It refines the believer by forcing him to expand his trust in God more and more. Suffering drives a believer to cast himself more and more upon the care of God; therefore, the believer moves closer and closer to the Lord praying, worshipping and fellowshipping with him more and more. God is in complete control of every situation. Sometimes He allows unpleasant trials to come our way, but this is all according to His will, according to His plan for our lives. We must trust God no matter what and do all we can to understand His will and to do it. **In fact, everyone who wants to live a godly life in Christ Jesus will be persecuted (2 Ti.3:12).** **For it has been granted to you on behalf of Christ not only to believe on him, but also to suffer for him (Ph.1:29).** **In this you greatly rejoice, though now for a little while you may have had to suffer grief in all kinds of trials. These have come so that your faith—of greater worth than gold, which perishes even though refined by fire—may be proved genuine and may result in praise, glory and honor when Jesus Christ is revealed (1 Pe.1:6-7).**

THE PROPHETS

PROPHET	TIME/PLACE GIVEN	MAIN MESSAGE	PRACTICAL APPLICATION
AHIJAH (Brother in Jehovah/Yahweh) **THE SHILONITE** **Known Facts** 1. Lived in Shiloh (1 K. 11:29). 2. Called to minister during the time of Solomon and Jeroboam (1 K.11:28-29). 3. Became blind in his old age (1 K.14:4). **Predictions and Messages** 1. The division of the nation of Israel into two kingdoms—the Northern Kingdom of Israel and the Southern Kingdom of Judah (1 K.11:31). 2. The death of Abijah, the son of King Jeroboam (1 K.14:9-13). 3. The destruction of the entire family of King Jeroboam (1 K. 14:10-13). 4. The captivity and exile of Israel to a foreign land (1 K. 14:14-16). **Scripture References** 1 K.11:29-39; 12:15; 14:4-16; 2 Chr.9:29	**Time** *The end of Solomon's reign, just before 931 B.C. until 910 B.C., near the end of the reign of Jeroboam I.* **Place** *Ahijah's first prophecy was given in the countryside, just outside Jerusalem.* *Later, after the division of the kingdom, Ahijah ministered in his hometown of Shiloh, preaching mainly to the Northern Kingdom of Israel.*	Israel was divided because the king and people had forsaken God, engaged in false worship, disobeyed God's commandments and refused to walk in the ways of the LORD. Jeroboam, Solomon's very own trusted servant, became king over the Northern Kingdom just as Ahijah predicted. But when King Jeroboam displayed a life of wickedness and idolatry, judgment fell on him and on his entire household, beginning with the immediate death of his own son. Eventually, all Israel would go into captivity, because they would not repent of their wickedness, nor turn from the state religion of idolatry and false worship instituted by Jerusalem. **Then he said to Jeroboam, "Take ten pieces for yourself, for this is what the LORD, the God of Israel, says: 'See, I am going to tear the kingdom out of Solomon's hand and give you ten tribes (1 K.11:31).** **You have done more evil than all who lived before you. You have made for yourself other gods, idols made of metal; you have provoked me to anger and thrust me behind your back." 'Because of this, I am going to bring disaster on the house of Jeroboam. I will cut off from Jeroboam every last male in Israel—slave or free. I will burn up the house of Jeroboam as one burns dung, until it is all gone...."As for you, go back home. When you set foot in your city, the boy will die....And the LORD will strike Israel, so that it will be like a reed swaying in the water. He will uproot Israel from this good land that he gave to their forefathers and scatter them beyond the River, because they provoked the LORD to anger by making Asherah poles (1 K. 14:9-10, 12, 15).**	If we continue in sin and wickedness and become involved in false worship, we will face the judgment of God. God will chastise and discipline us in order to bring us back to Him. God is zealous for us and will not allow us to chase after worldly affections, not for long. If we refuse to repent, we will face the judgment of God's hand. Even future generations may suffer and bear the brunt of our sins, suffering the great and terrible consequences of God's wrath. **If this is so, then the Lord knows how to rescue godly men from trials and to hold the unrighteous for the day of judgment, while continuing their punishment (2 Pe.2:9).** **He cuts off every branch in me that bears no fruit, while every branch that does bear fruit he prunes so that it will be even more fruitful (Jn.15:2).** **My son, do not despise the LORD's discipline and do not resent his rebuke, because the LORD disciplines those he loves, as a father the son he delights in (Pr. 3:11-12).** **You shall not bow down to them or worship them; for I, the LORD your God, am a jealous God, punishing the children for the sin of the fathers to the third and fourth generation of those who hate me, but showing love to a thousand [generations] of those who love me and keep my commandments (Ex.20:5-6).**

THE PROPHETS

PROPHET	TIME/PLACE GIVEN	MAIN MESSAGE	PRACTICAL APPLICATION
## AMOS (Burden-bearer) **Known Facts** 1. Lived in Tekoa, on the edge of the Judean desert (Am.1:1). 2. Worked as a shepherd and as a farmer of sycamore trees (Am.1:1; 7:14). 3. Wrote the book of *Amos*. 4. Preached fiery sermons and saw startling visions. **Predictions and Messages** 1. A sermon about God's coming judgment on sinful nations, including Israel (Am.1:1-4:13). 2. A sermon about the need for seeking God with the whole heart (Am.5:1-27). 3. A sermon warning the people not to be greedy (Am.6:4-14). 4. The vision of locusts—a picture of the crops being destroyed by the ferocious insects, but Amos interceded and God had mercy (Am.7:1-3). 5. The vision of fire—a picture of the fields being destroyed, but Amos interceded and God had mercy (Am.7:4-5). 6. The vision of a plumb line—a picture of the crookedness of Israel (Am.7:7-9). 7. The vision of a basket of fruit—a picture of the rottenness of Israel's sin (Am.8:1-3). 8. A sermon warning that God will severely judge those who treat the poor unfairly (Am.8:4-14). 9. The vision of the LORD standing on the altar, striking His own temple (Am.9:1-10). 10. The prophecy about the captivity and return of Israel (Am.9:9-15). **Scripture References** The book of *Amos*	**Time** *About 750 B.C., near the end of the rule of Jeroboam II in Israel and during the long reign of Uzziah in Judah.* *The time in which Amos preached was a very prosperous time economically and financially for the people of Israel, but not spiritually. Spiritually the hearts of the people were filled with greed, so much so that they oppressed the poor without mercy.* **Place** *Israel, the Northern Kingdom.*	God will judge sin wherever it is found. No sinner is exempt from judgment. Without genuine repentance, God's judgment will surely fall upon the sinner. Amos focused upon one theme, one subject: the coming judgment of God upon those who refused to turn from sin. Despite persecution and death threats, Amos faithfully continued to preach the messages given him by God, a series of blistering sermons against the sins of arrogance and pride. **"Therefore this is what I will do to you, Israel, and because I will do this to you, prepare to meet your God, O Israel" (Am.4:12).** **Amos answered Amaziah, "I was neither a prophet nor a prophet's son, but I was a shepherd, and I also took care of sycamore-fig trees. But the LORD took me from tending the flock and said to me, 'Go, prophesy to my people Israel' (Am.7:14-15).**	Worldly gain, such as riches, social position, heritage, even religion will not save a person. Such things can be good if they are used to help the poor or advance God's kingdom. But when a person uses worldly gain just for the purpose of more worldly gain, God's judgment is sure to fall upon that person. At least two major applications can be seen in the prophecies of Amos. 1. Just think of the people gripped by greed who push aside the needs of others... • to make themselves more comfortable • to buy some luxury • to enjoy more leisure time • to hoard more riches Shockingly, some people are so gripped by greed, they even assault and murder in order to gain more and more. Unbelievably, they consider human life worthless if it stands in the way of their gaining more riches. 2. The minister of God must boldly preach the Word of God. He must not form his sermon based on what people want to hear, nor avoid certain subjects because he will not be popular. The messenger of the LORD must be unashamed and unswerving in his calling to preach the whole counsel of God. Even persecution, no matter how serious, must not prevent the minister from proclaiming the Word of God, declaring what God has anointed him to say. **Command those who are rich in this present world not to be arrogant nor to put their hope in wealth, which is so uncertain, but to put their hope in God, who richly provides us with everything for our enjoyment (1 Ti.6:17).** **I thank God, whom I serve, as my forefathers did, with a clear conscience, as night and day I constantly remember you in my prayers. Recalling your tears, I long to see you, so that I may be filled with joy (2 Ti.1:3-4).**

PROPHET	TIME/PLACE GIVEN	MAIN MESSAGE	PRACTICAL APPLICATION
ANNA (Gracious) **Known Facts** 1. Served in the temple as a woman prophet (Lu.2:36). 2. Appeared as the first prophet since Malachi, a space of over 300 years. 3. Descended from the tribe of Asher (Lu. 2:36). 4. Widowed for many years (Lu.2:36). 5. Fasted and prayed continually (Lu.2:37). 6. Loved and hoped in God, therefore she was blessed (Lu.2:37). 7. Pointed out Christ to others (Lu.2:38). **Predictions and Messages** Jesus is the Christ, the Savior of the world (Lu.2:38). **Scripture References** Lu.2:36-38	**Time** *About 4 B.C., eight days after the birth of Jesus Christ.* **Place** *At the temple in Jerusalem.*	Anna's message was the greatest of all messages: Jesus Christ is the Redeemer, the promised Messiah Who brings redemption to all who ask for God's salvation. Anna shared this good news with anyone looking for redemption in Jerusalem. **Coming up to them at that very moment, she gave thanks to God and spoke about the child to all who were looking forward to the redemption of Jerusalem (Lu.2:38).**	1. God will greatly bless the person who places his entire hope in Him. God will always bless the person who trusts in Him. We must rely on God for our salvation, rely on Him with our whole heart, holding nothing back, seeking Him continually. For there is no other person, no other place, no other source to whom we can turn for the salvation of our soul. Salvation is in Christ, and Christ alone. 2. Believers should be busy talking to everyone about Jesus Christ, for Jesus Christ came to earth to redeem us from our sins. And He will grant forgiveness to anyone who seeks for it, to anyone who will place his entire hope in the Lord. **But the eyes of the LORD are on those who fear him, on those whose hope is in his unfailing love (Ps.33:18).** **And are justified freely by his grace through the redemption that came by Christ Jesus (Ro.3:24).**
ASAPH (Gathering) **Known Facts** 1. Was the son of Berechiah (1 Chr.6:39). 2. Descended from the tribe of Levi and the clan of Kohathites (1 Chr.6:33, 39). 3. Appointed by David as a musician, Asaph played the cymbals and sang (1 Chr. 6:31, 39). 4. Called a Seer (2 Chr. 29:30). 5. Wrote lyrics which were used many years after his death (2 Chr. 29:30). **Predictions and Messages** Sang and played music to praise and glorify the LORD. **Scripture References** 1 Chr.6:31-43; 15:17-19 2 Chr.29:30	**Time** *1004 B.C. Right after David was first crowned king in Hebron, he decided to bring the Ark of the Covenant from Kiriath-Jearim to Jerusalem. It was at this time that Asaph and the other musicians were appointed by King David to lead the people of Israel in worship, praising the LORD in songs of praise and celebration to the LORD.* **Place** *Jerusalem, the Holy City.*	Asaph was one of the leading musicians during the days of King David. Although there is not any specific message recorded by Asaph, he lived a life of praise and worship and greatly encouraged others to do so. Down through the years, Asaph's testimony was that of leading and encouraging the congregation in praising the LORD. **So the Levites appointed Heman son of Joel; from his brothers, Asaph son of Berekiah; and from their brothers the Merarites, Ethan son of Kushaiah (1 Chr.15:17).** **King Hezekiah and his officials ordered the Levites to praise the LORD with the words of David and of Asaph the seer. So they sang praises with gladness and bowed their heads and worshiped (2 Chr.29:30).**	The importance of praise and worship cannot be overstressed. As the Creator of the universe, the LORD expects us to praise and worship Him. It is the LORD Who has created life and Who sustains life. The air we breathe, the water we drink, the food we eat—every good and perfect gift we have comes from the hand of the LORD with Whom there is no changing. Because of all the richness and depth of all the blessings God pours out upon us—because of all the good and perfect gifts He so mercifully gives every day of our lives—the LORD expects, and rightly deserves, our worship and the praise of His holy name. **Let them give thanks to the LORD for his unfailing love and his wonderful deeds for men (Ps.107:8, 15, 21, 31).** **Praise be to the Lord, to God our Savior, who daily bears our burdens. Selah (Ps.68:19).**

PROPHET	TIME/PLACE GIVEN	MAIN MESSAGE	PRACTICAL APPLICATION
AZARIAH (Jehovah/Yahweh is my Helper) **Known Facts** 1. Was the son of Oded (2 Chr.15:1). 2. Ministered as the first of the prophets to the Southern Kingdom of Judah after the division of the nation of Israel. **Predictions and Messages** Azariah instructed King Asa to extend the revival which had begun in the land. Asa was not to lose courage, but to continue to serve God with fervor (2 Chr.15:2-7). **Scripture References** 2 Chr.15:1-12	**Time** *896 B.C., during the reign of Asa, king of Judah, who stirred a great reformation and revival among the people.* **Place** *Jerusalem, the Holy City and capital of Judah.*	Revival was sweeping through the land of Judah resulting in changed lives and a reformation of worship. King Asa and his troops had just delivered a crushing defeat to the invading Ethiopians. But right afterward, Asa was tempted to rely on his own strength. So Azariah, the prophet, pressed the king and the people to seek the LORD more than ever before. He challenged them not to fall into a foolish and destructive attitude of pride and self-reliance. Azariah declared that the LORD wanted the people to be as strong spiritually as they had been in battle. King Asa responded to Azariah's message and continued to stir a strong reformation among the people. He removed the pagan images of idolatry as well as those in charge of their worship. Then, he made all false worship illegal, instituting the death penalty for all who practiced it. Committing himself totally to the LORD, he established the purity of true worship, the worship of the LORD God alone (Jehovah/Yahweh). **The Spirit of God came upon Azariah son of Oded. He went out to meet Asa and said to him, "Listen to me, Asa and all Judah and Benjamin. The LORD is with you when you are with him. If you seek him, he will be found by you, but if you forsake him, he will forsake you.... But as for you, be strong and do not give up, for your work will be rewarded" (2 Chr.15:1-2, 7).**	Seeking the LORD is essential for every believer. We must seek Him with our whole heart, seek Him continually. Anything that could trap us in a deadly snare of sin must be removed. Placing God first in our lives, first in everything we do, must be our never-ending effort. We must draw close to the LORD, as close as we possibly can. We must continue to stoke the fire of revival in our hearts, to let it burn hotter and hotter. Why? Because we are always in need, in very desperate need, of God's help. Even when things seem to be going smoothly, we need God. We need Him... • for daily guidance • for spiritual strength • to escape temptation • for our daily food • to hold the world together • for our very next breath • for *all our needs, for every single need, every day of our lives* And remember this: God will *actively move in the behalf of the one who seeks Him.* Our labor is not in vain. There is a reward for serving God. God strongly supports those who wholeheartedly serve Him. **Let us not become weary in doing good, for at the proper time we will reap a harvest if we do not give up (Ga.6:9).** **But seek first his kingdom and his righteousness, and all these things will be given to you as well (Mt.6:33).** **For the eyes of the LORD range throughout the earth to strengthen those whose hearts are fully committed to him. You have done a foolish thing, and from now on you will be at war" (2 Chr.16:9).**

THE PROPHETS

PROPHET	TIME/PLACE GIVEN	MAIN MESSAGE	PRACTICAL APPLICATION
DANIEL **(God is my Judge)** **Known Facts** 1. Was taken captive by the Babylonians and forced to live in Babylon (Da.1:1-2). 2. Prophesied to three major world powers— Israel, Babylon and Medo-Persia (Da.1:1-2; 5:31). 3. Possessed tremendous integrity (Da. 1:8-10; 6:4; Eze.14:1). 4. Was given a Babylonian name (Belteshazzar) because he was highly favored among the exiles, and because he needed to conduct business in Babylon (Da.1:7). 5. Was able to understand all kinds of mysteries (Da.7:15-28; 8:15-27; 9:24-27; 10:1-14; Eze.28:3). 6. Was delivered miraculously from the den of lions (Da.6:19-23). 7. Saw strange and vivid visions about Israel's future, about the coming dominant world powers of human history, and about a future period of history known as the *Great Tribulation* and the end of the world (Da.7:1–12:13). 8. Wrote the book of *Daniel*. **Predictions and Messages** 1. The interpretation of King Nebuchadnezzar's dream of a great statue, which symbolizes the coming great world powers (Da.2:17-19). 2. The interpretation of King Nebuchadnezzar's dream of a great tree which predicted the coming judgment against Nebuchadnezzar due to his pride (Da.4:19-27). (Cont. on next page)	**Time** *605–535 B.C., during the Babylonian captivity of Judah and on into the first years of the Medo-Persian Empire. Daniel was just a young man, only about thirty years old when he was taken captive. He lived the rest of his days in Babylon, ministering to his people, serving as a statesman for Babylon and recording history, writing down his visions and prophecies of the future.* **Place** *Near the Tigris River during the last years of the Babylonian Empire and the first few years of the Medo-Persian Empire.*	The book of *Daniel* has one unmistakable message: God sets up kings and puts down kings. The powers of the world will struggle and struggle to gain domination, wealth, and control; but God is in control and over-rules everything they do, working all things out for the good of genuine believers and accomplishing His will for the world. Only He can exalt or humble; only He can deliver or destroy. God is sovereign over all. He lifts up those who acknowledge His sovereignty and puts down those who become filled with pride and self-sufficiency. After the end of the Assyrian Empire, control passed mainly to Babylon, which had been firmly established by Nabopolassar. Nabopolassar's son (Nebuchadnezzar II, the king we read about in the book of *Daniel*) then took over. The first thing Nebuchadnezzar did was to export most of the Judeans to Babylon. This included Daniel and his three friends. But despite their new pagan surroundings, Daniel and his three friends became very successful and were highly esteemed by the Babylonians. This was due to God's guidance, for they remained faithful to the LORD and to Him alone. Daniel became a close advisor and statesman for Nebuchadnezzar. Through the interpretation of dreams, which God inflicted upon the king, Daniel was lifted to a very high position in the Babylonian kingdom. Years later, Nebuchadnezzar's grandson Belshazzar became king. He was prideful like his grandfather before him. But there was a difference. Nebuchadnezzar repented and acknowledged God as the Sovereign over the earth, but Belshazzar refused to do so. The last straw came when Belshazzar defiled the articles of the temple of God by using them at a drunken feast in honor of a false god. At this, God literally wrote on the wall with His finger, burning a permanent message of immediate doom upon the king and the Babylonian empire. Belshazzar was slain that night as the Medo-Persian soldiers stormed the capital and the palace, and the new empire was put in place.	➤ All the world is to praise God for His holiness. ➤ All the world is to praise God for His sovereignty and omnipotence. ➤ All the world is to praise God for His eternal existence. What an indictment against man! How little we praise and worship God—truly praise and worship Him. Think for a moment and imagine in your mind the four beings who surround the throne of God. They were created to worship God, and they worship Him day and night, never ceasing from worshipping Him. They cry out day and night the glorious praise: "Holy, holy, holy, Lord God Almighty, which was, and is, and is to come" (Re. 4:8). The very thought of such a scene should bring us to our knees in repentance, humility and worship of God and His Son, Jesus Christ, the King of kings and Lord of lords. What a lesson the book of *Daniel* has for us! For the LORD God Almighty dwells in glory and majesty, dominion, and power. We owe Him our lives, all we are and have. **Exalt the LORD our God and worship at his holy mountain, for the LORD our God is holy (Ps.99:9).** **And they were calling to one another: "Holy, holy, holy is the LORD Almighty; the whole earth is full of his glory" (Is.6:3).** **Who will not fear you, O Lord, and bring glory to your name? For you alone are holy. All nations will come and worship before you, for your righteous acts have been revealed" (Re.15:4).** **I am the LORD who brought you up out of Egypt to be your God; therefore be holy, because I am holy (Lev.11:45).** **"I know that you can do all things; no plan of yours can be thwarted (Jb.42:2).** **Our God is in heaven; he does whatever pleases him (Ps.115:3).** **Yes, and from ancient days I am he. No one can deliver out of my hand. When I act, who can reverse it?" (Is.43:13).** **Jesus looked at them and said, "With man this is impossible, but with God all things are possible" (Mt.19:26).**

PROPHET	TIME/PLACE GIVEN	MAIN MESSAGE	PRACTICAL APPLICATION
DANIEL (cont.) 3. The message that God gives political power to whomever He wishes (Da.4:25). 4. The interpretation of the handwriting on the wall written to King Belshazzar by the finger of God Himself—the prediction of the soon coming judgment against Belshazzar and the end of the Babylonian Empire (Da.5:10-28). 5. The vision of the four beasts arising from the sea—a prophecy of the coming dominant world powers (Da.7:1-8). 6. The vision of Jesus Christ, the Ancient of Days (Da.7:9-10; Re.4:4; Mt.19:28; 1 Co.6:3). 7. The vision of the fourth beast being destroyed— the prophecy about the defeat of the antichrist (Da.7:11-12). 8. The vision of Jesus Christ—One like the Son of Man (Da.7:13-14). 9. The vision of the ram and the two horns— a prophecy of the end of the Medo-Persian Empire and the rise of the Greek Empire (Da.8:1-14). 10. The message from Gabriel about Jeremiah's seventy weeks— the prediction that the Messiah, Jesus Christ, the Savior of the world, would be rejected 483 years in the future (Da.9:24-26). 11. The message from Gabriel about Jeremiah's seventieth week— the prediction of the coming Tribulation, the desecration of the temple by the antichrist and the end of the world (Da.9:26-27; Mt.24:15-25; Mk.13:14-23). (Cont. on next page)		But Daniel, who continued to give God honor and to remain humble, was quickly lifted up to a high rank in the government of the Medes. Both before and after the change in power, Daniel saw amazing visions and received many startling messages from angels about the powers of the world, both present and future, and about the end times. Daniel wrote down many of these, but was instructed to withhold others. In all of his writings, Daniel continually proclaimed the great majesty of God and the need to honor Him. **"This was the dream, and now we will interpret it to the king. You, O king, are the king of kings. The God of heaven has given you dominion and power and might and glory; in your hands he has placed mankind and the beasts of the field and the birds of the air. Wherever they live, he has made you ruler over them all. You are that head of gold. "After you, another kingdom will rise, inferior to yours. Next, a third kingdom, one of bronze, will rule over the whole earth. Finally, there will be a fourth kingdom, strong as iron—for iron breaks and smashes everything—and as iron breaks things to pieces, so it will crush and break all the others. Just as you saw that the feet and toes were partly of baked clay and partly of iron, so this will be a divided kingdom; yet it will have some of the strength of iron in it, even as you saw iron mixed with clay. As the toes were partly iron and partly clay, so this kingdom will be partly strong and partly brittle. And just as you saw the iron mixed with baked clay, so the people will be a mixture and will not remain united, any more than iron mixes with clay. "In the time of those kings, the God of heaven will set up a kingdom that will never be destroyed, nor will it be left to another people. It will crush all those kingdoms and bring them to an end, but it will itself endure forever. This is the meaning of the vision of the rock cut out of a mountain, but not by human**	Now to him who is able to establish you by my gospel and the proclamation of Jesus Christ, according to the revelation of the mystery hidden for long ages past (Ro.16:25). I lift my hand to heaven and declare: As surely as I live forever (De.32:40). The eternal God is your refuge, and underneath are the everlasting arms. He will drive out your enemy before you, saying, 'Destroy him!' (De.33:27). Your name, O LORD, endures forever, your renown, O LORD, through all generations (Ps.135:13). "I am the Alpha and the Omega," says the Lord God, "who is, and who was, and who is to come, the Almighty" (Re.1:8). Yours, O LORD, is the greatness and the power and the glory and the majesty and the splendor, for everything in heaven and earth is yours. Yours, O LORD, is the kingdom; you are exalted as head over all (1 Chr.29:11). The LORD reigns, he is robed in majesty; the LORD is robed in majesty and is armed with strength. The world is firmly established; it cannot be moved (Ps.93:1). They will speak of the glorious splendor of your majesty, and I will meditate on your wonderful works (Ps.145:5). The seventh angel sounded his trumpet, and there were loud voices in heaven, which said: "The kingdom of the world has become the kingdom of our Lord and of his Christ, and he will reign for ever and ever" (Re.11:15).

PROPHET	TIME/PLACE GIVEN	MAIN MESSAGE	PRACTICAL APPLICATION
DANIEL (cont.) 12. The vision of the man dressed in linen standing by the Tigris River (Da.10:1-14). 13. The vision of the man who strengthened Daniel (Da.10:15-21). 14. The prophecy about the coming Greek Empire and Alexander the Great (Da.11:2-4). 15. The prophecies about the coming empires of Egypt and Syria and their struggle for world power (Da.11:5-35). 16. The prophecy of the distressing time at the end of the world—that those whose names are written in the Book of Life will be rescued (Da.12:1). 17. The prophecy of additional resurrections during the Tribulation (Da.12:2-3). **Scripture References** The book of *Daniel*		hands—a rock that broke the iron, the bronze, the clay, the silver and the gold to pieces. "The great God has shown the king what will take place in the future. The dream is true and the interpretation is trustworthy" (Da.2:36-45). How great are his signs, how mighty his wonders! His kingdom is an eternal kingdom; his dominion endures from generation to generation (Da. 4:3). At the end of that time, I, Nebuchadnezzar, raised my eyes toward heaven, and my sanity was restored. Then I praised the Most High; I honored and glorified him who lives forever. His dominion is an eternal dominion; his kingdom endures from generation to generation. All the peoples of the earth are regarded as nothing. He does as he pleases with the powers of heaven and the peoples of the earth. No one can hold back his hand or say to him: "What have you done?" (Da.4:34-35). "This is the inscription that was written: MENE, MENE, TEKEL, PARSIN "This is what these words mean: *Mene*: God has numbered the days of your reign and brought it to an end. *Tekel*: You have been weighed on the scales and found wanting. *Peres*: Your kingdom is divided and given to the Medes and Persians" (Da.5:25-28).	

PROPHET	TIME/PLACE GIVEN	MAIN MESSAGE	PRACTICAL APPLICATION
DAVID (Loved) **Known Facts** 1. Was the son of Jesse and the youngest of eight sons (1 S.16:11; 17:12). 2. Lived in Bethlehem (1 S.16:1; 17:12). 3. Descended from the tribe of Judah (Mt. 1:1-6). 4. Served the first king of Israel, King Saul, by playing music for him and by serving in Saul's army (1 S.16:23; 18:5). 5. Defeated the giant Goliath as a youth (1 S.17). 6. Was anointed king over all Israel and reigned forty years (1 S.16:1,11-13; 2 S.5:5). 7. Was promised by God that the Savior would come through his lineage (Mt.1:1-17). 8. Wrote 73 Psalms (Ps. 22:1; 23:1; 41:1; 110:1). 9. Played musical instruments in praise to the LORD (2 S.23:2). 10. Was a brilliant military leader and strategist. Led great military campaigns (1 S. 18:5-7). 11. Had a heart that was like the heart of God (1 S.13:14; Ac.13:22). **Predictions and Messages** 1. The Messiah, the Savior of the world, would be a priest after the order of Melchizedek (Ps.110:4; Mt. 27:50-51; Mk. 15:37-38; Lu.23:44-46; He.6:20). 2. The Messiah would be betrayed by a friend (Ps.41:9; Mt. 26:20-25; Mk.14:10-11; Lu.22:2-6; Jn. 13:1-2; 1 Co.11:23). 3. The Messiah's betrayer would be removed from office and replaced (Ps. 109:7-8; Ac.1:18-20). (Cont. on next page)	**Time** *1029–971 B.C. All his life, King David sang and wrote psalms (songs) to the LORD. In his times of rejoicing and in his time of despair, David cried out to God in beautiful songs of poetry.* **Place** *Many places throughout Judea and Samaria as well as southern Jerusalem, the City of David.*	David was a shining example of trust in God, of placing his life in the palm of God's hand. Whenever David was in trouble, he turned to God as His Savior, trusting the LORD completely for deliverance. And the LORD always saved, delivered David because of the saving acts of God and in his behalf, David was able to write many heartfelt Psalms that are recorded in the Holy Scripture. And God was able to use David to predict many of the prophecies about Jesus Christ hundreds of years before the Savior was born. **These are the last words of David: "The oracle of David son of Jesse, the oracle of the man exalted by the Most High, the man anointed by the God of Jacob, Israel's singer of songs: "The Spirit of the LORD spoke through me; his word was on my tongue (2 S.23:1-2).**	David trusted fully that God would do exactly as He had promised, that He would send the promised King and Savior to establish His throne forever in the world. The confessions of David's heart were made in simple trust, arising from a heart that was truly convinced that God does exactly what He says He will do. David's trust is a dynamic example for us, for it is simple trust God desires from man—nothing more and nothing less. We simply must rely on God. We must lean on Him with our whole heart, put our complete trust in the LORD to do exactly as He says. The LORD will save those who trust in Him. **My God is my rock, in whom I take refuge, my shield and the horn of my salvation. He is my stronghold, my refuge and my savior—from violent men you save me (2 S.22:3).** **But let all who take refuge in you be glad; let them ever sing for joy. Spread your protection over them, that those who love your name may rejoice in you (Ps.5:11).** **O LORD my God, I take refuge in you; save and deliver me from all who pursue me (Ps.7:1).** **The LORD redeems his servants; no one will be condemned who takes refuge in him (Ps.34:22).** **Let the morning bring me word of your unfailing love, for I have put my trust in you. Show me the way I should go, for to you I lift up my soul (Ps.143:8).**

PROPHET	TIME/PLACE GIVEN	MAIN MESSAGE	PRACTICAL APPLICATION
DAVID (cont.) 4. The Messiah, the Savior of the world, would be falsely accused (Ps. 27:12; 35:11; Mt. 26:59-62; Mk. 14:55-59). 5. The Messiah would be hated for no reason (Ps.69:4; Jn.15:23-25). 6. The Messiah's hands and feet would be pierced (Ps.22:16; Jn. 20:25-27). 7. The Messiah would bear the sins of the world (Ps.22:1; Mt. 27:45-46; Mk.15:33-34). 8. The Messiah would be mocked (Ps.22:6-8; Mt.27:39-40; Mk. 15:29-32; Lu.23:35-37). 9. The Messiah would be given gall and vinegar (Ps.69:21; Mt. 27:48; Mk.15:36; Jn. 19:28-29). 10. The Messiah would pray for His enemies (Ps.109:4; Lu.23:34). 11. The Messiah's garments would be gambled for (Ps.22:18; Mt.27:35; Mk.15:24; Lu.23:34; Jn.19:23-25). 12. The Messiah would not have any broken bones (Ps.34:20; see Ex. 12:46; Jn.19:31-37). 13. The Messiah would be resurrected (Ps. 16:10; Mt.12:39-41; 16:4; 28:1-7; Mk. 16:1-8; Lu.11:29-32; 24:1-8; Jn.20:1-8). 14. The Messiah would ascend to heaven (Ps. 68:18; Mk.16:19-20; Lu.24:50-51; Ac.1:6-9; Ep.4:8-10). **Scripture References** 1 S.16–1 K. 2; Ps.16, 22, 27, 34, 41, 68, 69, 109, 110			

THE PROPHETS

PROPHET	TIME/PLACE GIVEN	MAIN MESSAGE	PRACTICAL APPLICATION
DEBORAH (Honey bee) **Known Facts** 1. Was married to Lapidoth (Jud.4:4). 2. Judged Israel, deciding civil cases for the people according to God's Word (Jud. 4:4). 3. Wrote a song of deliverance after the defeat of Sisera and the Canaanite army (Jud.5). **Predictions and Messages** 1. Barak was to gather ten thousand men from Naphtali and Zebulun, and God would deliver Sisera into his hand (Jud.4:4-8). 2. Sisera would be killed by a woman because Barak refused to go without Deborah (Jud.4:9). **Scripture References** Jud.4-5	**Time** *Approximately 1220 B.C., during a time of oppression by King Jabin of the Canaanites. It was about 200 plus years before King David and about 200 plus after the Exodus.* **Place** *Between Ramah and Bethel, in the hill country of Ephraim.*	The LORD is a mighty Deliverer, Who will deliver Israel from the Canaanite enemies. Through Deborah, God instructed Barak to mobilize ten thousand troops and to meet the enemy commander Sisera, at the Kishon River. Gripped by fear and feeling inadequate for the task, Barak refused to go without Deborah's help. Granting his request, God used both Deborah and Barak to soundly defeat the oppressing Canaanites in a tremendous victory. But because Barak refused to obey God, he was denied the honor of capturing the enemy commander Sisera. Instead, the honor of killing the dreaded enemy commander was given to a woman name Jael. **She sent for Barak son of Abinoam from Kedesh in Naphtali and said to him, "The LORD, the God of Israel, commands you: 'Go, take with you ten thousand men of Naphtali and Zebulun and lead the way to Mount Tabor. I will lure Sisera, the commander of Jabin's army, with his chariots and his troops to the Kishon River and give him into your hands.'" Barak said to her, "If you go with me, I will go; but if you don't go with me, I won't go." "Very well," Deborah said, "I will go with you. But because of the way you are going about this, the honor will not be yours, for the LORD will hand Sisera over to a woman." So Deborah went with Barak to Kedesh (Jud.4:6-9).**	The courage of Deborah stands as a dynamic example for us all. Just imagine—facing a massive army unarmed! Deborah courageously accepted this challenge, but not Barak. He was reluctant, fainthearted, fearful, and unbelieving. From this experience of Deborah and Barak, we must learn one lesson: there is no room in the service of God for being fainthearted, fearful, or unbelieving. God commands us to be courageous, to step forth and face the enemy with courage and boldness, No matter what the enemy or its power, we are to be courageous in standing against it. God promises to help us and to deliver us if we will confront the enemy courageously in His name. Have I not commanded you? Be strong and courageous. Do not be terrified; do not be discouraged, for the LORD your God will be with you wherever you go" (Jos.1:9). The wicked man flees though no one pursues, but the righteous are as bold as a lion (Pr.28:1). So do not fear, for I am with you; do not be dismayed, for I am your God. I will strengthen you and help you; I will uphold you with my righteous right hand (Is.41:10).

THE PROPHETS

PROPHET	TIME/PLACE GIVEN	MAIN MESSAGE	PRACTICAL APPLICATION
ELIEZER (God is my Helper) **Known Facts** 1. Was the son of Doda-vah (2 Chr. 20:37). 2. Lived in Mareshah (2 Chr.20:37). **Predictions and Messages** Rebuked King Jehosha-phat for forming an alliance with an evil king, King Ahaziah of the Northern Kingdom of Israel (2 Chr.20:37). **Scripture References** 2 Chr.20:35-37	**Time** *849-48 B.C., at the end of the reign of Jehosha-phat, king of Judah.* **Place** *Jerusalem, the capital of the Southern Kingdom of Judah.*	Eliezer rebuked King Jehosha-phat of Judah for making an agreement with the evil King Ahaziah of the Northern Kingdom of Israel. Eliezer declared that God had caused their gold-seeking ships to be destroyed because God was so displeased with Jehosha-phat's actions. **Later, Jehoshaphat king of Judah made an alliance with Ahaziah king of Israel, who was guilty of wickedness. He agreed with him to construct a fleet of trading ships. After these were built at Ezion Geber, Eliezer son of Dodavahu of Mareshah prophesied against Jehosha-phat, saying, "Because you have made an alliance with Ahaziah, the LORD will destroy what you have made." The ships were wrecked and were not able to set sail to trade (2 Chr.20:35-37).**	God warns the believer against compromising and forming world-ly alliances with the unbelievers and wicked people of this world. God demands spiritual separation. For if we fellowship, closely asso-ciate with the sinful and wicked of this earth, eventually we will be seduced to join in and participate in their sin. Compromise is forbid-den by God. We are to live lives of spiritual separation, not compro-mising our commitment to God, not engaging in the sinful and wicked behavior of unbelievers. **"Be careful, or your hearts will be weighed down with dissipa-tion, drunkenness and the anxi-eties of life, and that day will close on you unexpectedly like a trap (Lu.21:34).** **Therefore, I urge you, broth-ers, in view of God's mercy, to offer your bodies as living sacri-fices, holy and pleasing to God—this is your spiritual act of wor-ship. Do not conform any longer to the pattern of this world, but be transformed by the renewing of your mind. Then you will be able to test and approve what God's will is—his good, pleasing and perfect will (Ro.12:1-2).** **But now I am writing you that you must not associate with an-yone who calls himself a brother but is sexually immoral or greedy, an idolater or a slander-er, a drunkard or a swindler. With such a man do not even eat (1 Co.5:11).**

THE PROPHETS

PROPHET	TIME/PLACE GIVEN	MAIN MESSAGE	PRACTICAL APPLICATION
ELIJAH (Yahweh is God) **Known Facts** 1. Was from Tishbi (1 K.17:1). 2. Lived in Gilead (1 K.17:1). 3. Ministered to the Northern Kingdom of Israel (1 K.17:1). 4. Performed many miracles: ➤ Prevented rain for three years (1 K.17:1; Js.5:17). ➤ Multiplied flour and oil during the entire time of the drought (1 K.17:14). ➤ Raised a child from the dead (1 K.17:22). ➤ Called fire down from heaven (1 K.18:38; 2 K.1:10). ➤ Brought rain (1 K.18:41). ➤ Divided the Jordan River and crossed on dry ground (2 K.2:8). **Predictions and Messages** 1. A long, severe drought would come to Israel (1 K.17:1). 2. The flour and oil of the widow of Zarepath would multiply miraculously so that she would have an unending daily supply as long as the drought continued (1 K.17:14). 3. A torrential rain would come to end the long drought (1 K.18:41). 4. The blood of Ahab would be licked up by the dogs to avenge the blood of Naboth (1 K. 21:19; 2 K.9:24-26). 5. The household of Ahab would be destroyed and come to a complete end (1 K.21:21-24). **Scripture References** 1 K.17–2 K.2	**Time** *860-845 B.C., during the reigns of Ahab, Ahaziah, and Jehoram, kings of Northern Israel.* **Place** *The Northern Kingdom of Israel.*	For over three years, Elijah predicted that it would not rain. Through this terrible drought, Elijah was able to warn the people time and again against the false worship of Baal. Baal was thought to be the god of the weather and fertility, and the worship of this false god was strongly encouraged by King Ahab and Queen Jezebel. But with fervor and stunning miracles, God called people to repentance through Elijah's ministry. Finally, a showdown was held between Elijah and the false prophets of Baal, a confrontation that was to prove once and for all who the real God was. Perhaps no scene in the Old Testament is more dramatic than when Elijah called down fire from heaven upon his sacrifice on Mt. Carmel. The spectacular, miraculous event proved once for all that Jehovah/Yahweh is the One True God, the only real and living God. Sadly, despite this tremendous display of God's power, Ahab and the people still did not repent. **Now Elijah the Tishbite, from Tishbe in Gilead, said to Ahab, "As the LORD, the God of Israel, lives, whom I serve, there will be neither dew nor rain in the next few years except at my word" (1 K.17:1).** **For this is what the LORD, the God of Israel, says: 'The jar of flour will not be used up and the jug of oil will not run dry until the day the LORD gives rain on the land'" (1 K.17:14).** **And Elijah said to Ahab, "Go, eat and drink, for there is the sound of a heavy rain" (1 K.18:41).** **I will make your house like that of Jeroboam son of Nebat and that of Baasha son of Ahijah, because you have provoked me to anger and have caused Israel to sin' (1 K.21:22).**	1. The LORD (Jehovah, Yahweh) is the One and only living and true God: there is no other God. All false gods are just this: false. They are nonexistent, not really living, not possessing life. They are powerless, unable to respond. Being lifeless, they cannot hear prayers, nor reach out to help us in our desperate hours of need. False gods are totally incapable of being present with us as we walk day by day. They are unable to guide us or to fulfill any promise ever made by a false prophet. All other so-called gods are false. They exist only in a person's imagination. 2. If a person refuses to believe God's Word, he will not believe nor follow the Lord, even if he sees a dramatic sign from heaven. **"I am the Alpha and the Omega," says the Lord God, "who is, and who was, and who is to come, the Almighty" (Re.1:8).** **Do not tremble, do not be afraid. Did I not proclaim this and foretell it long ago? You are my witnesses. Is there any God besides me? No, there is no other Rock; I know not one" (Is.44:8).** **"He said to him, 'If they do not listen to Moses and the Prophets, they will not be convinced even if someone rises from the dead'" (Lu.16:31).**

PROPHET	TIME/PLACE GIVEN	MAIN MESSAGE	PRACTICAL APPLICATION
ELISHA (God is the Savior) **Known Facts** 1. Was the son of Shaphat (1 K.19:16). 2. Lived in Abel-Meholah (1 K.19:16). 3. Was anointed by Elijah to take his place, as God instructed (1 K.19:16). 4. Performed many miracles: ➤ Parted the Jordan River (2 K.2:14). ➤ Made bitter water sweet (2 K.2:19-22). ➤ Saved an army by causing water to appear in ditches (2 K.3:13-20). ➤ Multiplied the widow's oil (2 K.4:1-7). ➤ Raised a child from the dead (2 K.4:32-37). ➤ Purified a pot of food from poison (2 K.4:38-41). ➤ Multiplied bread and grain to feed one hundred men (2 K.4:42-44). ➤ Healed a leper (2 K.5:1-14). ➤ Caused an ax head to float in the Jordan River (2 K.6:1-7). ➤ Raised a man from the dead, when the man came in contact with Elisha's bones (2 K.13:21). 5. Prophesied in the Northern Kingdom (2 K. 2:2). 6. Saw Elijah transported to heaven (2 K.2:9-13). 7. Was the model of a spiritual leader (1 K. 19:19-21; 2 K.5:16). (Cont. on next page)	**Time** *850–795 B.C., during the reigns of Jehoram, Jehu, Jehoahaz, and Jehoash, kings of Northern Israel.* **Place** *Israel, The Northern Kingdom of Israel.*	God will save those who have faith in Him. Time and time again, in both the words and deeds of Elisha, this message of salvation was demonstrated. Elisha had strong faith in God and faithfully followed God. But he not only followed, he demonstrated an iron determination in living a godly, righteous life. Elisha's life was a beacon, a bright example to everyone he met. Persevering to his very last day on earth, he repeatedly demonstrated the saving, miraculous power of God. **Then he went out to the spring and threw the salt into it, saying, "This is what the LORD says: 'I have healed this water. Never again will it cause death or make the land unproductive'" (2 K.2:21).** **For this is what the LORD says: You will see neither wind nor rain, yet this valley will be filled with water, and you, your cattle and your other animals will drink (2 K.3:17).** **"How can I set this before a hundred men?" his servant asked. But Elisha answered, "Give it to the people to eat. For this is what the LORD says: 'They will eat and have some left over'" (2 K.4:43).** **But Elisha said to him, "Was not my spirit with you when the man got down from his chariot to meet you? Is this the time to take money, or to accept clothes, olive groves, vineyards, flocks, herds, or menservants and maidservants? Naaman's leprosy will cling to you and to your descendants forever." Then Gehazi went from Elisha's presence and he was leprous, as white as snow (2 K.5:26-27).** **Elisha said, "Hear the word of the LORD. This is what the LORD says: About this time tomorrow, a seah of flour will sell for a shekel and two seahs of barley for a shekel at the gate of Samaria." The officer on whose arm the king was leaning said to the man of God, "Look, even if the LORD should open the floodgates of the heavens, could this happen?" "You will see it with your own eyes," answered Elisha, "but you will not eat any of it!" (2 K.7:1-2).**	Far too often men and women demonstrate traits of weak character, traits such as insincerity, deception, impurity, dishonesty, corruption and wickedness. Whereas they should be living lives of honor, goodness, purity, morality, and sincerity. This is not the way any of us should be living. We should be men and women of honor and uprightness, holding ever so high the principles of morality, righteousness and justice for all people everywhere. We should be followers of Christ, and we should persevere, be steadfast in our faith. Once we profess Christ, we must continue to profess and follow after Him. *Continuing on* is the evidence of our faith. When people see us continuing to follow Christ, they know that our profession is true. But if we profess to be a follower of the LORD and then refuse to live like He says, people know that we are making a false profession. We must *continue on,* being steadfast, enduring, persevering in following Christ—this assures our salvation, that our profession is true, that our life demonstrates what we say. **Come back to your senses as you ought, and stop sinning; for there are some who are ignorant of God—I say this to your shame (1 Co.15:34).** **because you know that the Lord will reward everyone for whatever good he does, whether he is slave or free (Ep.6:8).** **But you, man of God, flee from all this, and pursue righteousness, godliness, faith, love, endurance and gentleness. Fight the good fight of the faith. Take hold of the eternal life to which you were called when you made your good confession in the presence of many witnesses (1 Ti.6:11-12).** **It teaches us to say "No" to ungodliness and worldly passions, and to live self-controlled, upright and godly lives in this present age, while we wait for the blessed hope—the glorious appearing of our great God and Savior, Jesus Christ (Tit.2:12-13).** **Worship the LORD your God, and his blessing will be on your food and water. I will take away sickness from among you (Ex.23:25).**

PROPHET	TIME/PLACE GIVEN	MAIN MESSAGE	PRACTICAL APPLICATION
ELISHA (cont.) **Predictions and Messages** 1. The water of a spring would be purified, will be sweet (2 K. 2:21). 2. Water would miraculously appear in some trenches especially prepared by faith to catch the water (2 K.3:17). 3. Food would be multiplied (2 K.4:43). 4. Gehazi and his descendants would be struck with leprosy (2 K.5:26-27). 5. A great famine would end in one day (2 K.7:1). 6. The king's attendant would see the end of the famine, but would not eat any of the food because he did not believe the Word of the LORD (2 K. 7:2). 7. Jehu would become king and kill the entire family of Ahab (2 K.9:6-8). 8. The prediction that Israel would have three victories over Syria (2 K.13:14-19). **Scripture References** 1 K.19:16-19; 2 K.2–13		Jehu got up and went into the house. Then the prophet poured the oil on Jehu's head and declared, "This is what the LORD, the God of Israel, says: 'I anoint you king over the LORD's people Israel. You are to destroy the house of Ahab your master, and I will avenge the blood of my servants the prophets and the blood of all the LORD's servants shed by Jezebel. The whole house of Ahab will perish. I will cut off from Ahab every last male in Israel—slave or free (2 K.9:6-8).	He does not take his eyes off the righteous; he enthrones them with kings and exalts them forever (Jb.36:7). The eyes of the LORD are on the righteous and his ears are attentive to their cry (Ps.34:15). I was young and now I am old, yet I have never seen the righteous forsaken or their children begging bread (Ps.37:25).

THE PROPHETS

PROPHET	TIME/PLACE GIVEN	MAIN MESSAGE	PRACTICAL APPLICATION
EZEKIEL **(God is strong)** **Known Facts** 1. Was the son of Buzi (Eze.1:3). 2. Served as a priest in the temple (Eze.1:3). 3. Wrote the book of *Ezekiel* (Eze.1:1-3). 4. Was taken captive into Babylon (Eze. 1:2; 2 K.24:11-16). 5. Called to be a watchman to the people of Israel (Eze. 3:17). 6. Called to be a sign or symbol to the people of Israel (Eze.12:6, 11; 24:21-27). **Predictions and Messages** 1. Visions of the glory of the LORD and Ezekiel's calling (Eze.1–3). 2. Prophecies concerning Judah and Jerusalem—that God would judge and send the people into captivity because they profaned the holy temple (Eze.4–24). 3. Prophecies concerning other nations—that God would judge their sin, especially Egypt, but Israel will be restored (Eze.25–32). 4. Prophecies concerning the restoring of Israel—that Israel would be restored when the people repented and turned back to the LORD (Eze.33–39). 5. A vision and a detailed description of the future temple and of heaven (Eze.40–48). **Scripture References** The book of *Ezekiel*	**Time** *593–571 B.C., before and during the final captivity and exile of Judah and Jerusalem in 586 B.C.* **Place** *Ezekiel first prophesied in Jerusalem, but later was taken captive into Babylon. In Babylon (or the land of the Chaldeans), Ezekiel was sitting next to the River Chebar when the Spirit of God revealed to him strange and wonderful visions of the glory of the LORD and of heaven (Eze.1:3).*	"Know that I am the LORD." This main message of Ezekiel occurs sixty-three times throughout the book of *Ezekiel*. Ezekiel's messages strongly emphasized the holiness of God, and the fact that God will judge sin. But the LORD will also forgive and restore those who repent and turn to Him. God is known by His judgment; but He is better known by His mercy. Throughout his ministry, Ezekiel was greatly persecuted and eventually killed for his straightforward preaching. But he stood fast, unswervingly preaching the messages the LORD laid upon his heart. **"When any Israelite or any alien living in Israel separates himself from me and sets up idols in his heart and puts a wicked stumbling block before his face and then goes to a prophet to inquire of me, I the LORD will answer him myself. I will set my face against that man and make him an example and a byword. I will cut him off from my people. Then you will know that I am the LORD (Eze.14:7-8).** **And they will know that I am the LORD; I did not threaten in vain to bring this calamity on them (Eze.6:10).** **"But if a wicked man turns away from all the sins he has committed and keeps all my decrees and does what is just and right, he will surely live; he will not die (Eze.18:21).** **Say to them, 'As surely as I live, declares the Sovereign LORD, I take no pleasure in the death of the wicked, but rather that they turn from their ways and live. Turn! Turn from your evil ways! Why will you die, O house of Israel?' (Eze.33:11).**	Despite the love of God, people shockingly reject the LORD. This is why God judges and shows His wrath. Man is without excuse. Man has no defense, no answer, no reason that can justify his rebellion against God. Yet God is merciful to the person who repents. He gave His Son to die for us. We do not deserve it—we never have and we never will—but God loves us with an incomprehensible love. Therefore, He has given His Son to die *for* us, as our substitute, in our behalf. But a person must accept the gift of God's Son, accept Jesus Christ by true faith and repentance in order to receive God's mercy. **Let the wicked forsake his way and the evil man his thoughts. Let him turn to the LORD, and he will have mercy on him, and to our God, for he will freely pardon (Is.55:7).** **Therefore tell the people: This is what the LORD Almighty says: 'Return to me,' declares the LORD Almighty, 'and I will return to you,' says the LORD Almighty (Zec. 1:3).**

PROPHET	TIME/PLACE GIVEN	MAIN MESSAGE	PRACTICAL APPLICATION
GAD (Fortunate) **Known Facts** 1. Recorded some of the history of King David (1 Chr.29:29-30). 2. Ministered as a prophet for many years. 3. Served by the side of King David and King Solomon as the king's seer (2 Chr.29:25). **Predictions and Messages** 1. Warned David to flee from Judah whenever Saul was about to find him (1 S.22:5). 2. Announced God's judgment for David's sin of numbering the people (2 S.24:10-15; 1 Chr.21:9-13). 3. Gave instructions to David for ending the severe plague of judgment on the people (2 S. 24:18-19; 1 Chr. 21:18-19). **Scripture References** 1 S.22:4; 2 S.24:11-19; 1 Chr.9-19; 2 Chr.29:25	**Time** *1015–950 B.C., before the division of the nation of Israel.* **Place** *Jerusalem and certain areas to the south, while he served by the side of King David and King Solomon.*	Our strength and security is in the LORD. No amount of human ability or might can keep us safe—only God can. So as we face the trials, temptations and enemies of life, we must remain humble before the LORD, never allowing ourselves to become puffed up with pride, thinking that we have some great ability or resource to conquer the hardships and sufferings of life. It is never by our own strength, but God's that we triumph in life. **So he left them with the king of Moab, and they stayed with him as long as David was in the stronghold. But the prophet Gad said to David, "Do not stay in the stronghold. Go into the land of Judah." So David left and went to the forest of Hereth (1 S.22:4-5).** **See, my father, look at this piece of your robe in my hand! I cut off the corner of your robe but did not kill you. Now understand and recognize that I am not guilty of wrongdoing or rebellion. I have not wronged you, but you are hunting me down to take my life. May the LORD judge between you and me. And may the LORD avenge the wrongs you have done to me, but my hand will not touch you. As the old saying goes, 'From evildoers come evil deeds,' so my hand will not touch you (2 S.24:11-13).** **Then the angel of the LORD ordered Gad to tell David to go up and build an altar to the LORD on the threshing floor of Araunah the Jebusite. So David went up in obedience to the word that Gad had spoken in the name of the LORD....David said to him, "Let me have the site of your threshing floor so I can build an altar to the LORD, that the plague on the people may be stopped. Sell it to me at the full price."...David built an altar to the LORD there and sacrificed burnt offerings and fellowship offerings. He called on the LORD, and the LORD answered him with fire from heaven on the altar of burnt offering. Then the LORD spoke to the angel, and he put his sword back into its sheath (1 Chr.21:18-19, 22, 26-27).**	A spirit of pride, conceit, and haughtiness is a terrible evil. For when we exalt ourselves, we walk around acting as though we are better, more capable, more deserving, more moral, more righteous than someone else. But note this inescapable truth: we reap what we sow. If we sow prideful sin and evil, we reap the consequences. So it is with any act of wickedness. This is a spiritual law set up by God for the purpose of divine judgment. A person may repent, but the wickedness will result in some consequence of suffering. **Pride goes before destruction, a haughty spirit before a fall (Pr.16:18).** **Do not be deceived: God cannot be mocked. A man reaps what he sows (Ga.6:7).** **With him is only the arm of flesh, but with us is the LORD our God to help us and to fight our battles." And the people gained confidence from what Hezekiah the king of Judah said (2 Chr.32:8).** **He who trusts in himself is a fool, but he who walks in wisdom is kept safe (Pr.28:26).**

THE PROPHETS

PROPHET	TIME/PLACE GIVEN	MAIN MESSAGE	PRACTICAL APPLICATION
HABAKKUK **(Tightly embraced)** **Known Facts** 1. Ministered to Judah, the Southern Kingdom. 2. Wrote the book of *Habakkuk* (Hab.1:1). **Predictions and Messages** 1. The oracle of the wickedness of the people (Hab.1:1-4). 2. The oracle of the shocking invasion of the Chaldeans (Hab. 1:5-17). 3. The answer of God to Habakkuk's plea—the wicked will be judged, but the righteous will live by faith (Hab.2:1-20). 4. The prayer of Habakkuk—the LORD is glorious and mighty (Hab.3:1-16). 5. The praise of Habakkuk—the LORD protects those who trust in Him even in the midst of trouble and distress (Hab.3:17-20). **Scripture References** The book of *Habakkuk*; Ro.1:17; Ga.3:11-12; He.10:37-38	**Time** *615-598 B.C., during the reigns of Jehoahaz and Jehoiakim, about 20 years before the captivity of Judah and Jerusalem.* **Place** *Judah, the Southern Kingdom.*	The heart of Habakkuk ached to the point of breaking. The prophet was in anguish for three reasons. First, Habakkuk saw the horrible wickedness of Israel, the deep sin of his own people. Second, he knew that the terrible judgment of God's hand was coming because of Israel's sin. Third, and what weighed most heavily on his soul, Habakkuk longed to be acceptable before the holy God Whom he served. In his book, Habakkuk recorded several question he asked of God and the LORD's answer to his questions. After humbly pleading and lamenting to the LORD, Habakkuk waited (for the prophet never presumed, not even for a moment, that God is unjust). He simply asked his questions and then waited for the LORD to change his heart, so that he could fully trust Him. Among the LORD's answer to Habakkuk is the vital message found in Hab.2:4. This important verse teaches us that we must guard against pride and trust in God. Habakkuk faithfully preached this message, longing for his people to listen and repent. **Therefore the law is paralyzed, and justice never prevails. The wicked hem in the righteous, so that justice is perverted (Hab.1:4).** **I am raising up the Babylonians, that ruthless and impetuous people, who sweep across the whole earth to seize dwelling places not their own (Hab.1:6).** **"See, he is puffed up; his desires are not upright—but the righteous will live by his faith (Hab.2:4).** **God came from Teman, the Holy One from Mount Paran.** *Selah* **His glory covered the heavens and his praise filled the earth (Hab.3:3).** **The Sovereign LORD is my strength; he makes my feet like the feet of a deer, he enables me to go on the heights (Hab.3:19).**	God's chosen way for us to approach Him is that we "live by faith." After all, Scripture declares as clearly as it can: no man is justified by the law in the sight of God. God is perfect; He is perfectly righteous. No man can achieve perfection; therefore, no man can live in the presence of God. No matter how good he is or how much good he does, he cannot achieve perfection. The fact is evident, for if a man had achieved perfection, he would be perfect—living forever in a perfect state of being, even on this earth. But note this: What God does is take a person's faith and count that faith as righteousness, as perfection. Therefore, a man is able to live in God's presence by faith or justification. The point is this: God's way for a man to approach Him is the way of faith: "The just shall live by faith." **And without faith it is impossible to please God, because anyone who comes to him must believe that he exists and that he rewards those who earnestly seek him (He.11:6).** **Let the heavens rejoice, let the earth be glad; let them say among the nations, "The LORD reigns!" (1 Chr.16:31).** **God reigns over the nations; God is seated on his holy throne (Ps.47:8).** **Do not let your heart envy sinners, but always be zealous for the fear of the LORD (Pr.23:17).** **I know that everything God does will endure forever; nothing can be added to it and nothing taken from it. God does it so that men will revere him (Ec.3:14).**

22

PROPHET	TIME/PLACE GIVEN	MAIN MESSAGE	PRACTICAL APPLICATION
HAGGAI (Feast of Yahweh) **Known Facts** 1. Ministered to Judah, the Southern Kingdom. 2. Wrote the book of *Haggai* (Hag.1:1). **Predictions and Messages** 1. The declaration that it is time to build the temple of the LORD (Hag.1:2). 2. A sermon about taking courage because the LORD is with you (Hag.2:4). 3. The foretelling of the future blessing of Israel by the LORD (Hag.2:19). 4. The prophecy that Zerubbabel will be lifted up as a leader (Hag.2:23). **Scripture References** The book of *Haggai*; Ezr.5:1; 6:14	**Time** *520 B.C., when the second foundation of the temple was to be laid.* **Place** *Jerusalem, the Holy City and place of the temple.*	Haggai's messages were given to encourage and strengthen the returned exiles of Jerusalem as they sought to rebuild their temple and nation. He taught that the Spirit of the LORD mightily dwells among those who reverence and honor Him. The citizens of Jerusalem at this time had just returned from captivity in Babylon. Although they were in their own land, it was new and unfamiliar because it was their ancestors, not them, who had been taken captive seventy years before. Naturally, the people were glad to be free. But they still felt somewhat discouraged, unsure of what to do next. They were a people without direction. Through the prophet Haggai, the LORD gave special direction and greatly encouraged the people. Haggai told of a bright future and promised a strong leader in Zerubbabel. Most of all, the Spirit of the LORD would be among the people if they would honor the LORD and give Him their true heartfelt worship. **This is what the LORD Almighty says: "These people say, 'The time has not yet come for the LORD's house to be built'" (Hag.1:2).** **But now be strong, O Zerubbabel,' declares the LORD. 'Be strong, O Joshua son of Jehozadak, the high priest. Be strong, all you people of the land,' declares the LORD, 'and work. For I am with you,' declares the LORD Almighty (Hag.2:4).** **Is there yet any seed left in the barn? Until now, the vine and the fig tree, the pomegranate and the olive tree have not borne fruit. "'From this day on I will bless you'" (Hag.2:19).** **"'On that day,' declares the LORD Almighty, 'I will take you, my servant Zerubbabel son of Shealtiel,' declares the LORD, 'and I will make you like my signet ring, for I have chosen you,' declares the LORD Almighty" (Hag.2:23).**	How many of us have little rituals, prayers, habits, ceremonies, and objects that we use to keep us religiously secure? So many of us seek religious security while at the same time we neglect the weightier matter of breaking God's Law. It is not the man-made place or the man-made ritual that saves a person. What saves a person is coming to God in true worship, bowing before Him, acknowledging Him as God, acknowledging that His Son, Jesus Christ, is the only way and the only hope of salvation. The place of worship is no longer the temple or any other particular location on earth. God's presence now dwells in the hearts and lives of His people. His people worship Him wherever they are, and they can worship Him every day all day long. True worship means that we focus on the object of worship, being sure that we are truly worshipping the Father, God Himself. A person may be in a fancy, expensive church or in a broom closet worshipping, and yet not be worshipping the Father. A man's whole being must be focused upon the only true and living God, worshipping Him and Him alone. God desires worship, for He created man to worship and fellowship with Him. Therefore, man needs to truly worship God. Man needs to worship God with the spiritual drive and ability of his soul, seeking the most intimate communion and fellowship with God. Man needs to worship God with the spiritual core of his life and being, trusting and resting in God's acceptance and love and care. **Praise the LORD. How good it is to sing praises to our God, how pleasant and fitting to praise him! (Ps.147:1).** **Yet you are enthroned as the Holy One; you are the praise of Israel (Ps.22:3).** **Let us rejoice and be glad and give him glory! For the wedding of the Lamb has come, and his bride has made herself ready (Re.19:7).** **Praise the LORD. Sing to the LORD a new song, his praise in the assembly of the saints (Ps.149:1).** **Glorify the LORD with me; let us exalt his name together (Ps.34:3).**

PROPHET	TIME/PLACE GIVEN	MAIN MESSAGE	PRACTICAL APPLICATION
HANANI (Merciful) **Known Facts** 1. Ministered to Judah, the Southern Kingdom (2 Chr.16:7). 2. Father of Jehu, the prophet (1 K.16:1-7). **Predictions and Messages** 1. The declaration that it was foolish for King Asa to rely on anyone other than the LORD (2 Chr.16:7-9). 2. The declaration that the LORD supports those who completely rely on Him (2 Chr. 16:9). **Scripture References** 2 Chr.16:7-10	**Time** *870 B.C., at the end of the reign of Asa, king of Judah, and just after King Asa made a treaty with the Arameans (Syrians).* **Place** *Jerusalem, in the palace of the king.*	We must rely totally on the LORD, and our dependence upon Him must not be passive. Rather, we must *actively seek* to trust the LORD more and more. For He searches the earth seeking people who are totally committed to Him. His eyes scan back and forth, looking for people who will place their lives fully into His hands. Furthermore, He longs to meet their needs and to strengthen and deliver them from all the hardships and temptations of life. But the people of Judah failed to actively trust and seek the Lord. Consequently, they were to suffer the judgment of God. **At that time Hanani the seer came to Asa king of Judah and said to him: "Because you relied on the king of Aram and not on the LORD your God, the army of the king of Aram has escaped from your hand. Were not the Cushites and Libyans a mighty army with great numbers of chariots and horsemen? Yet when you relied on the LORD, he delivered them into your hand. For the eyes of the LORD range throughout the earth to strengthen those whose hearts are fully committed to him. You have done a foolish thing, and from now on you will be at war" (2 Chr.16:7-9).**	Note the wonderful promise of Scripture: God works through the events of this world to meet the needs of His dear people, those who are fully committed to Him. No matter how terrible the trial or temptation, God moves within the event for one purpose and one purpose only: to deliver and to strengthen those who are fully committed to Him. A person who is fully committed can rest assured in this promise of the Lord. For the Lord will provide, protect and guide His dear people. Even in the moment of death, the Lord will transfer us into His presence—quicker than the eye can blink (2 Ti.4:18). **One thing I ask of the LORD, this is what I seek: that I may dwell in the house of the LORD all the days of my life, to gaze upon the beauty of the LORD and to seek him in his temple (Ps.27:4).** **The Lord will rescue me from every evil attack and will bring me safely to his heavenly kingdom. To him be glory for ever and ever. Amen (2 Ti.4:18).** **So do not fear, for I am with you; do not be dismayed, for I am your God. I will strengthen you and help you; I will uphold you with my righteous right hand (Is.41:10).** **And the God of all grace, who called you to his eternal glory in Christ, after you have suffered a little while, will himself restore you and make you strong, firm and steadfast (1 Pe.5:10).**

PROPHET	TIME/PLACE GIVEN	MAIN MESSAGE	PRACTICAL APPLICATION
HEMAN (Faithful) **Known Facts** 1. Was the son of Joel (1 Chr.15:17). 2. Served as the seer to King David (1 Chr. 25:5). 3. Appointed by David to lead the congregational music (1 Chr. 25:1). 4. Born into the tribe of Levi (1 Chr.24:31). 5. Prophesied along with his family through the music (1 Chr. 25:1-8). **Predictions and Messages** None recorded. Since he is called a *seer,* he must have sung some of the LORD's predictions through the music of worship, as well as advised David about the results of certain royal decisions. **Scripture References** 1 Chr.25:1-8	**Time** 971 *B.C., the last days of the life of King David. In these solemn times of final instructions from King David, Levites were assigned the task of making sure the worship of the LORD continued down through coming generations.* **Place** *Jerusalem, the Holy City.*	Heman praised the LORD with music and greatly encouraged the congregation of Israel in their worship of God. Leading music was his official position under King David. Heman prophesied while playing musical instruments. Just as Asaph, Heman's father, had faithfully served under King David, now Heman, Asaph's son, carried on the work. Heman carried the legacy of his father, praising the LORD with music and spurring the people on in their devotion to the LORD. **David, together with the commanders of the army, set apart some of the sons of Asaph, Heman and Jeduthun for the ministry of prophesying, accompanied by harps, lyres and cymbals. Here is the list of the men who performed this service....As for Heman, from his sons: Bukkiah, Mattaniah, Uzziel, Shubael and Jerimoth; Hananiah, Hanani, Eliathah, Giddalti and Romamti-Ezer; Joshbekashah, Mallothi, Hothir and Mahazioth. All these were sons of Heman the king's seer. They were given him through the promises of God to exalt him. God gave Heman fourteen sons and three daughters. All these men were under the supervision of their fathers for the music of the temple of the LORD, with cymbals, lyres and harps, for the ministry at the house of God. Asaph, Jeduthun and Heman were under the supervision of the king (1 Chr.25:1, 4-6).**	The importance of praise and worship cannot be overstressed. Because of all His good and perfect gifts—the LORD expects us to worship and praise His holy name. Music is one way, a very powerful way, to give praise to the Lord. We are to be talking about Christ, admonishing others in the Word of God and singing within our hearts the hymns of the church. We are to walk about rejoicing and praising the Lord within our hearts, being filled with the joy of the Lord and His Word, and bearing strong testimony for the Lord. **Let the word of Christ dwell in you richly as you teach and admonish one another with all wisdom, and as you sing psalms, hymns and spiritual songs with gratitude in your hearts to God (Col.3:16).**

PROPHET	TIME/PLACE GIVEN	MAIN MESSAGE	PRACTICAL APPLICATION
HOSEA (Salvation) **Known Facts** 1. Was the son of Beeri (Ho.1:1) 2. Prophesied for many years, his ministry extending through the reign of four kings (Ho.1:1). 3. Ministered to both the Northern and Southern Kingdoms (Ho.1:1). **Predictions and Messages** 1. The illustrated sermon about Hosea's unfaithful wife (Ho. 1:1–3:5). 2. The sermon about God's case against Israel, that they were full of sin and that they must repent (Ho.4:1–6:3). 3. The sermon about God's certain judgment of sin (Ho.6:4–10:15). 4. The sermon about God's love for Israel, even though they were rebellious (Ho. 11:1–13:16). 5. The prophecy that Christ would come out of Egypt (Ho. 11:1; Mt.2:15). 6. The sermon about God's call to repentance (Ho.14:1-3). 7. The promise of God's blessing coming upon the people (Ho.14:4-8). 8. The sermon about God's challenge to the wise listener (Ho.14:9). *Scripture References* The book of *Hosea* (Cont. on next page)	**Time** *788–723 B.C., during the reigns of four Judean kings: Uzziah, Jotham, Ahaz, and Hezekiah. His ministry spawned the reigns of the last six kings of the Northern Kingdom, but he did not name these rulers. His ministry ended just before the fall of Samaria in 722 B.C.* **Place** *Both the Northern and Southern Kingdoms.*	Hosea had a hard life. He was given a very unusual command from God: to marry a prostitute. Hosea's life was an illustrated sermon of the unfaithfulness of the people, and how they had turned away from God. During the course of their marriage, Gomer (Hosea's wife) bore three children to Hosea, two of them fathered by someone else. Once, Hosea had to go to the public auction and buy his wife back from slavery. The shame of the situation was unbearable, which was the very message preached to the people. Israel should have been... • ashamed at the way they had been acting • ashamed at the way they had run away from the LORD • ashamed at the way they had gone after the lust of their flesh • ashamed at the way they had failed to serve God, in particular after all He had done for them Hosea preached bold, straightforward messages to the people, warning them that they must repent from their sin and seek the LORD. The people had been committing spiritual adultery against the LORD, running after the pleasures and the false gods of the world, pleasing their carnal nature. They needed to allow the LORD to break through the callousness of their hearts, for their souls were as unyielding as dry ground that had not been plowed. Otherwise, the hand of God's judgment would chastise them. But even in chastisement, God's people must remember that God disciplines His people. **"Come, let us return to the LORD. He has torn us to pieces but he will heal us; he has injured us but he will bind up our wounds. After two days he will revive us; on the third day he will restore us, that we may live in his presence. Let us acknowledge the LORD; let us press on to acknowledge him. As surely as the sun rises, he will appear; he will come to us like the winter rains, like the spring rains that water the earth" (Ho.6:1-3).**	God disciplines believers. He chastens, corrects, and rebukes believers. Now God does not cause bad and evil in life. God loves man. Therefore, God's concern is not to cause problems and pain for us; His concern is to deliver us through all the trouble and pain on earth and to save us for heaven and eternity. How does God do this? By chastising us. When we think of chastisement, we usually think of discipline and correction and it does mean this. But it also means to train and teach and instruct a person. Every true child of God knows the discipline of God's hand. His discipline differs with each of us, but each of us can recognize His discipline nevertheless. God stirs, guides, directs, teaches, trains, and instructs us all along the way, making us stronger and stronger in life and drawing us closer and closer to Him. **I will be like the dew to Israel; he will blossom like a lily. Like a cedar of Lebanon he will send down his roots; his young shoots will grow. His splendor will be like an olive tree, his fragrance like a cedar of Lebanon (Ho.14:5-6).** **So that you may become blameless and pure, children of God without fault in a crooked and depraved generation, in which you shine like stars in the universe (Ph.2:15).** **"Submit to God and be at peace with him; in this way prosperity will come to you (Jb.22:21).** **I have been crucified with Christ and I no longer live, but Christ lives in me. The life I live in the body, I live by faith in the Son of God, who loved me and gave himself for me (Ga.2:20).**

PROPHET	TIME/PLACE GIVEN	MAIN MESSAGE	PRACTICAL APPLICATION
HOSEA (cont.)		When I please, I will punish them; nations will be gathered against them to put them in bonds for their double sin. Ephraim is a trained heifer that loves to thresh; so I will put a yoke on her fair neck. I will drive Ephraim, Judah must plow, and Jacob must break up the ground. Sow for yourselves righteousness, reap the fruit of unfailing love, and break up your unplowed ground; for it is time to seek the LORD, until he comes and showers righteousness on you. But you have planted wickedness, you have reaped evil, you have eaten the fruit of deception. Because you have depended on your own strength and on your many warriors (Ho.10:10-13).	

PROPHET	TIME/PLACE GIVEN	MAIN MESSAGE	PRACTICAL APPLICATION
HULDAH (Life) **Known Facts** 1. Was the wife of Shallum, the keeper of the wardrobe (2 K. 22:14). 2. Lived in the Second Quarter of Jerusalem (2 K.22:14). **Predictions and Messages** 1. The prophecy that God would judge Jerusalem for idolatry, for ignoring God's Word (2 K.22:14-17; 2 Chr.34:22-25). 2. The prophecy that God would be kind to King Josiah, because Josiah had humbled himself, recognizing the sin of the people and the importance of heeding God's Word (2 K.22:18-20; 2 Chr. 34:26-28). **Scripture References** 2 K.22:14-20; 2 Chr. 34:22-28	**Time** *623 B.C., the eighteenth year of Josiah's reign, when King Josiah decided to repair the temple and a copy of the Law of Moses was found during the renovations.* **Place** *Jerusalem, the capital of Judah, the Southern Kingdom of Israel.*	King Josiah gave specific instructions to repair the temple of the LORD. While the repairs were being made, a copy of the Law was found in the temple. King Josiah read the Word of God and was aghast at what he read, because he realized that the people had grossly neglected the law and disobeyed the LORD's commandments. Earnestly wanting to understand what he had read, he commissioned a delegation of officials to seek a prophet who could explain God's Word to him. The delegation went to Huldah the prophetess who gave the following explanation: the penalties for disobeying the laws found written in the Book were to be executed, because the people had forsaken the LORD, worshipped false gods, and provoked the LORD to anger. God was going to judge and destroy the city of Jerusalem. But despite the terrifying message of judgment spoken by Huldah, the LORD had a very special message for King Josiah. Josiah had grieved over the people's sin, and he had humbled himself before the LORD in prayer and personal repentance. Because Josiah's heart was tender and responsive to the Word of God, Josiah would not personally experience the terrible judgment. It would come after Josiah's death. **She said to them, "This is what the LORD, the God of Israel, says: Tell the man who sent you to me, 'This is what the LORD says: I am going to bring disaster on this place and its people, according to everything written in the book the king of Judah has read. Because they have forsaken me and burned incense to other gods and provoked me to anger by all the idols their hands have made, my anger will burn against this place and will not be quenched.' Tell the king of Judah, who sent you to inquire of the LORD, 'This is what the LORD, the God of Israel, says concerning the words you heard: Because your heart was responsive and you humbled yourself before the LORD when you heard what I have spoken against this place and its people, that they would become accursed and laid waste, and because** (Cont. in col. 4)	What a lesson for us! To Josiah and his people, the Word of God had been lost. To many of us, the Word of God is neglected and ignored, even denied and rejected. Some of us act as though we do not believe the Bible is the written Word of God. After all, if we truly believed that the Bible is God's Word, we would read, study and feast upon it. The Bible truly is what it claims to be, God's Word; and if we ignore it and neglect it, what will God say to us when we face Him? Above all that is to be feared in this life is the neglect or denial of God and His Holy Word. Nothing on this earth is as important as doing exactly what God's Word says, obeying Him and keeping His commandments. But before we can keep His commandments, we must know what His commandments are. And there is only one way to learn God's commandments: study His Holy Word. **You diligently study the Scriptures because you think that by them you possess eternal life. These are the Scriptures that testify about me (Jn.5:39).** **Now the Bereans were of more noble character than the Thessalonians, for they received the message with great eagerness and examined the Scriptures every day to see if what Paul said was true (Ac.17:11).** **Do your best to present yourself to God as one approved, a workman who does not need to be ashamed and who correctly handles the word of truth (2 Ti.2:15).** (cont. from col.3) **you tore your robes and wept in my presence, I have heard you, declares the LORD. Therefore I will gather you to your fathers, and you will be buried in peace. Your eyes will not see all the disaster I am going to bring on this place.'" So they took her answer back to the king (2 K.22:15-20).**

PROPHET	TIME/PLACE GIVEN	MAIN MESSAGE	PRACTICAL APPLICATION
IDDO (Appointed) **Known Facts** 1. Recorded some history about Solomon, Rehoboam, and Abijah (2 Chr.9:29). 2. Called a seer by the Scripture, a seer to whom God gave special vision against the wickedness and false worship of Jeroboam I (2 Chr.9:29). 3. Kept genealogical records (2 Chr.12:15). 4. Was not the "Iddo" who was the father of Zechariah the prophet. **Predictions and Messages** Wrote about the rebuke of Jeroboam given by the unnamed prophet at Bethel (1 K.13:1-5). **Scripture References** 2 Chr.9:29; 12:15; 13:22	**Time** *910 B.C., after the close of the ministry of Ahijah, the Shilonite, and after the reign of Jeroboam I, who put the idols of the golden calves at Dan and Bethel.* **Place** *Judah, the Southern Kingdom of Israel.*	Iddo was appointed by God to keep a record of Jeroboam's terrible wickedness and false worship and of the unknown prophets who rebuked the king. How did Iddo know about these events? The Scripture expressly states that Iddo was given special visions concerning Jeroboam (2 Chr.9:29). It should be noted that the unnamed prophet who gave the rebuke to Jeroboam did not remain faithful. He forgot God's Word and went off on his own, doing what he thought was right instead of following God's clear instructions. Apparently, because of the prophet's unfaithfulness, God later raised up Iddo to record the event so the world would have a permanent warning against the wickedness and the false worship of Jeroboam I. The unnamed prophet who cursed the altar at Bethel could not have been Iddo the seer because the unnamed prophet was killed before returning home (1 K.13:24). **As for the other events of Solomon's reign, from beginning to end, are they not written in the records of Nathan the prophet, in the prophecy of Ahijah the Shilonite and in the visions of Iddo the seer concerning Jeroboam son of Nebat? (2 Chr.9:29).** **As for the events of Rehoboam's reign, from beginning to end, are they not written in the records of Shemaiah the prophet and of Iddo the seer that deal with genealogies? There was continual warfare between Rehoboam and Jeroboam (2 Chr.12:15).** **The other events of Abijah's reign, what he did and what he said, are written in the annotations of the prophet Iddo (2 Chr.13:22).**	Accountability is clearly taught in Scripture. The Lord is coming; and when He comes, He will judge the works of His servant and followers. All works of the believer will be inspected by the Lord so that each believer may be rewarded in perfect justice, receiving exactly what is due, whether good or bad (2 Co. 5:10). **So you also must be ready, because the Son of Man will come at an hour when you do not expect him. "Who then is the faithful and wise servant, whom the master has put in charge of the servants in his household to give them their food at the proper time? It will be good for that servant whose master finds him doing so when he returns (Mt.24:44-46).** **Now it is required that those who have been given a trust must prove faithful (1 Co.4:2).** **Each one should use whatever gift he has received to serve others, faithfully administering God's grace in its various forms (1 Pe.4:10).** **Therefore, my dear brothers, stand firm. Let nothing move you. Always give yourselves fully to the work of the Lord, because you know that your labor in the Lord is not in vain (1 Co.15:58).** **Watch your life and doctrine closely. Persevere in them, because if you do, you will save both yourself and your hearers (1 Ti.4:16).**

PROPHET	TIME/PLACE GIVEN	MAIN MESSAGE	PRACTICAL APPLICATION
ISAIAH **(Salvation is from the LORD)** **Known Facts** 1. Was the son of Amoz (Is.1:1). 2. Ministered alongside Hosea the prophet. 3. Saw a tremendous vision of the LORD (Is.6). 4. Prophesied more about the Messiah than any other prophet. **Predictions and Messages** 1. A holy group of people will remain after the captivity (Is. 6:11-13). 2. Christ, the Savior of the world, will live among men on the earth (Is.7:13-16). 3. Foreign armies will quickly invade and smash Samaria (Is.8:1-4). 4. Christ will be the Wonderful Counselor (Is.9:1-7). 5. The Savior will come from the family of David (Is.11:1-6). 6. Judgment will come on wicked nations (Is.13:1–20:6). 7. The Servant of the LORD will come on a mission of mercy (Is.42:1-9). 8. A remnant of God's people will be gathered back to the promised land (Is. 43:1–45:25). 9. King Cyrus, who would help Israel many years later to return to the promised land, is called by name (Is. 45:1-13). 10. Yahweh is the only Savior (Is.45:18-25). 11. Babylon will fall (Is.47:1–48:15). 12. Christ will be the Suffering Servant and die an atoning death (Is.52:13–53:12). 13. An everlasting covenant will be given to Israel (Is.55:3-5). (cont. in col.4) **Scripture References** The book of *Isaiah*, 2 K.18–20	**Time** *740–690 B.C., during the reigns of Uzziah, Jotham, Ahaz, and Hezekiah.* **Place** *Jerusalem, the capital city of Judah.*	Isaiah's prophecies and sermons centered on the holiness of God and His desire to save mankind from his sin. Spurred on by his dramatic and unforgettable vision of God's holy throne, he warned people of coming disaster. But he also had many words of comfort to say from the LORD. Most importantly, Isaiah prophesied of the coming Savior, Who would bear the punishment for the sins of the world. But the main message of Isaiah is the same as the meaning of his name: "Salvation is from the LORD." It is essential to understand this biblical truth. For it is not just that salvation comes from the LORD (Jehovah/Yahweh) the One True God; but that salvation *only* comes from the LORD. It *only* comes through Jesus Christ, the Son of God, the Messiah whom the Father sent into the world to give His life as a ransom for the world. There is no other that can save. Only the LORD can rescue man from his desperately sinful situation. **Surely God is my salvation; I will trust and not be afraid. The LORD, the LORD, is my strength and my song; he has become my salvation" (Is.12:2).** **In that day they will say, "Surely this is our God; we trusted in him, and he saved us. This is the LORD, we trusted in him; let us rejoice and be glad in his salvation" (Is.25:9).** **Declare what is to be, present it—let them take counsel together. Who foretold this long ago, who declared it from the distant past? Was it not I, the LORD? And there is no God apart from me, a righteous God and a Savior; there is none but me. "Turn to me and be saved, all you ends of the earth; for I am God, and there is no other (Is.45:21-22).** **But he was pierced for our transgressions, he was crushed for our iniquities; the punishment that brought us peace was upon him, and by his wounds we are healed (Is.53:5).**	The way to God is through Jesus Christ Himself. Jesus Christ alone saves, for there is no other exalted Lord. Therefore, no man can be saved by any other name other than the Lord's name. No teacher is capable enough, no prophet is noble enough, no minister is good enough to save himself, much less anyone else. Therefore, no matter the claim and no matter the strength of a person's name, no man has the name by which God can save people. All men are mortal. Therefore, no man can make another man immortal. But the Name which God uses to save men is eternal, the Name of the Lord Jesus Christ, the Son of God Himself. **Jesus answered, "I am the way and the truth and the life. No one comes to the Father except through me (Jn.14:6).** **Salvation is found in no one else, for there is no other name under heaven given to men by which we must be saved" (Ac.4:12).** **Predictions and Messages** (cont. from col.1) 14. A Messiah will come to save (Is.61:1-11). 15. A description of the Millennium (Is.66:14-24).

THE PROPHETS

PROPHET	TIME/PLACE GIVEN	MAIN MESSAGE	PRACTICAL APPLICATION
JACOB/ISRAEL (Deceiver/Contender with God) **Known Facts** 1. Was the son of Isaac, son of Abraham (Ge. 25:19-26). 2. Fathered twelve sons, who became the heads of the twelve tribes of Israel (Ex.1:1-7). 3. Tricked his brother, Esau, into giving him the birthright; thus, the Messiah, the Savior of the world, came through Jacob's family (Ge.25:27-34). 4. Tricked his father, Isaac, into giving him the blessing of the firstborn, taking it from his brother, Esau (Ge.27:30-40). **Predictions and Messages** Jacob prophesied about the future of his twelve sons. The most important of all these prophetic utterances is that the Messiah, the Savior of the world, would come from the tribe of Judah. **Scripture References** Ge.48–49	**Time** *1858 B.C., after Jacob and his sons had sojourned in Egypt 17 years and more than 400 years before the Exodus.* **Place** *Goshen, a territory in the land of Egypt that was ruled by Pharaoh Sunusret III.*	In the later years of Jacob's life, he predicted the future of his twelve sons. His sons were to become the twelve tribes of Israel; consequently, Jacob was predicting the future of the nation of Israel and ultimately of the Savior to come, Jesus Christ. Although Jacob was not ordinarily a prophet, while on his deathbed, Jacob was anointed by God's Spirit to prophesy. The most important part of what Jacob predicted had to do with his son Judah. Judah would be the tribe from which the Messiah would arise. **The scepter will not depart from Judah, nor the ruler's staff from between his feet, until he comes to whom it belongs and the obedience of the nations is his (Ge.49:10).**	Just think of this wonderful fact: God had a plan to save us before the world was ever made. How marvelous is God's love. And so that there would be no mistake, God revealed His plan in His Holy Word. God outlined very specific facts about Jesus Christ so that it would be clear that He is the Messiah, Son of God, and Savior of the world. Note just six of the essential facts, facts that clearly teach that Jesus Christ is the promised Seed, the Savior of the world: ➤ Jesus Christ is "the Lion of the tribe of Judah" (Re.5:5). ➤ Jesus Christ is the Prince of peace (Is.9:6). ➤ Jesus Christ gives rest to the human soul (Mt.11:29). ➤ Jesus Christ came to the earth so that we might have life, abundant life (Jn.10:10). ➤ Jesus Christ is the Savior and lord of the world and all owe their obedience to Him (Is.45:22-23; Ph.2:9-11). ➤ Jesus Christ came and gave His life on the cross for the redemption of humankind, and He will return again to gather His people unto Himself (Mk.13:27; Jn.14:1-3; 1 Th.4:16-18). **Then one of the elders said to me, "Do not weep! See, the Lion of the tribe of Judah, the Root of David, has triumphed. He is able to open the scroll and its seven seals" (Re.5:5).** **Therefore God exalted him to the highest place and gave him the name that is above every name, that at the name of Jesus every knee should bow, in heaven and on earth and under the earth, and every tongue confess that Jesus Christ is Lord, to the glory of God the Father (Ph.2:9-11).**

31

THE PROPHETS

PROPHET	TIME/PLACE GIVEN	MAIN MESSAGE	PRACTICAL APPLICATION
JAHAZIEL **(God sees me)** **Known facts** 1. Was a Levite (2 Chr. 20:14). 2. Was the son of Zechariah (not the prophet) (2 Chr. 20:14). 3. Descended from the lineage of Asaph (2 Chr. 20:14). 4. Served during the reign of Jehoshaphat (2 Chr.20:15). **Predictions and Messages** Prophesied that the LORD Himself would defeat the foreign coalition that was coming to attack (2 Chr. 20:15-17). **Scripture References** 2 Chr.20:14-18	**Time** *860 B.C., in the middle of the reign of Jehoshaphat and during the ministry of Elijah in the Northern Kingdom.* **Place** *Jerusalem, in the courtyard of the house of the LORD.*	During the reign of King Jehoshaphat, a coalition of three nations joined together to attack Judah. Instead of turning to foreign alliances as he had done in the past, Jehoshaphat prayed to God for help. As he waited for an answer, the Spirit of the LORD came upon Jahaziel, a Levite standing in the courtyard. Jahaziel prophesied that the LORD Himself would defeat the enemy (2 Chr.20:15-17). The next day when Judah went out to battle, they discovered the vast army of enemy soldiers lying dead all over the ground. During the night the LORD had apparently stirred the enemy soldiers to argue and fight among themselves. The result was catastrophic; and the enemy coalition, in a state of utter confusion, attacked and slaughtered each other. All Judah had to do was pick up the spoils. God had worked a wonderful miracle to rescue Judah and King Jehoshaphat (2 Chr.20:20-30). **Then the Spirit of the LORD came upon Jahaziel son of Zechariah, the son of Benaiah, the son of Jeiel, the son of Mattaniah, a Levite and descendant of Asaph, as he stood in the assembly. He said: "Listen, King Jehoshaphat and all who live in Judah and Jerusalem! This is what the LORD says to you: 'Do not be afraid or discouraged because of this vast army. For the battle is not yours, but God's. Tomorrow march down against them. They will be climbing up by the Pass of Ziz, and you will find them at the end of the gorge in the Desert of Jeruel. You will not have to fight this battle. Take up your positions; stand firm and see the deliverance the LORD will give you, O Judah and Jerusalem. Do not be afraid; do not be discouraged. Go out to face them tomorrow, and the LORD will be with you'" (2 Chr.20:14-17).**	The lesson for us is a much needed one on the importance of prayer and fasting. Jehoshaphat and his people faced an overwhelming crisis, a crisis that they stood no chance of getting through—at least not successfully. Within their own strength, they would have been crushed. Therefore, they did the only thing they could do: they turned to the LORD. In order to show the LORD how sincere and desperate they were, they set aside a full day for fasting and prayer. They showed the LORD the depth of their sincerity, that they were willing to repent, to turn away from their sins and recommit their lives to Him anew. What a dynamic lesson for us! When we face a severe crisis, we too must seek to show the sincerity of our hearts and the depth of our need through fasting and prayer. We must commit ourselves to the LORD. Simply stated, seeking God through prayer and fasting is the way to secure the presence and power of the LORD. When we face a crisis or are longing for more of God's blessings, we should fast and pray often, showing the depth of our sincerity. **"Watch and pray so that you will not fall into temptation. The spirit is willing, but the body is weak" (Mt.26:41).** Yet when they were ill, I put on sackcloth and humbled myself with fasting. When my prayers returned to me unanswered (Ps.35:13).

PROPHET	TIME/PLACE GIVEN	MAIN MESSAGE	PRACTICAL APPLICATION
JEHU (Jehovah/Yahweh is He) **Known Facts** 1. Was the son of Hanani the seer (1 K.16:1). 2. Was not the king whom Elijah and Elisha anointed to be king of Israel and to execute the LORD's vengeance upon the household of Ahab. 3. Recorded history about some of the kings of Israel (2 Chr.20:34). **Predictions and Messages** 1. The family of King Baasha would be completely destroyed because of his terrible idolatry (1 K.16:1-3). 2. The wrath of the LORD would be upon Jehoshaphat because of the evil alliance he had made with King Ahab. However, because Jehoshaphat had removed the wicked idols of Ashtoreth, the LORD also saw the good in Jehoshaphat's heart (2 Chr. 19:2-3). **Scripture References** 1 K.16:1-3, 12; 2 Chr. 19:1-3	**Time** *886 B.C., at the end of the reign of Baasha, king of Israel, to 853 B.C., during the reign of Jehoshaphat, king of Judah—the year Jehoshaphat made an alliance with the evil King Ahab of Israel.* **Place** *Samaria, the northern capital, in 886 B.C.; Jerusalem, the southern cap-ital in 853 B.C.*	Before Israel conquered the land of Canaan, the LORD had strongly given them two warnings. First, they were to drive out the Canaanites completely and without mercy so that the evil of idolatry would not creep into the pure worship of the LORD. Second, they were not to intermarry with the heathen nations. The message of Jehu rekindled the fire of God's warning that had been given down through the centuries. But as before, His warnings through Jehu were not heeded. King Baasha followed after the false gods of idolatry. And King Jehoshaphat intermarried with the family of Ahab and Jezebel in order to form an alliance. God was angry because these kings, the leaders of His people, had rejected and disobeyed His Holy Word. They had ignored God's written message, so God raised up Jehu the prophet to once again warn the leaders and people: they must obey God's Word or face the judgment of God. **Then the word of the LORD came to Jehu son of Hanani against Baasha: "I lifted you up from the dust and made you leader of my people Israel, but you walked in the ways of Jeroboam and caused my people Israel to sin and to provoke me to anger by their sins. So I am about to consume Baasha and his house, and I will make your house like that of Jeroboam son of Nebat (1 K.16:1-3).** **Jehu the seer, the son of Hanani, went out to meet him and said to the king, "Should you help the wicked and love those who hate the LORD? Because of this, the wrath of the LORD is upon you. There is, however, some good in you, for you have rid the land of the Asherah poles and have set your heart on seeking God" (2 Chr.19:2-3).**	God expects His followers to love everyone, even the wicked and those who hate God and His followers (Mt.5:44). But while loving and reaching out to the unbelievers of the world, the believer must never compromise his testimony for the LORD. He must never act against God's Word, disobeying the commandments of the LORD. He must always live a life of spiritual separation, a life that does not fellowship or form alliances with unbelievers. The believer must always take a stand for righteousness against wickedness. **But now I am writing you that you must not associate with anyone who calls himself a brother but is sexually immoral or greedy, an idolater or a slanderer, a drunkard or a swindler. With such a man do not even eat (1 Co.5:11).** **If anyone comes to you and does not bring this teaching, do not take him into your house or welcome him. Anyone who welcomes him shares in his wicked work (2 Jn.10-11).** **Be careful not to make a treaty with those who live in the land where you are going, or they will be a snare among you (Ex.34:12).** **Blessed is the man who does not walk in the counsel of the wicked or stand in the way of sinners or sit in the seat of mockers (Ps.1:1).**

THE PROPHETS

PROPHET	TIME/PLACE GIVEN	MAIN MESSAGE	PRACTICAL APPLICATION
JEREMIAH (Yahweh will rise up) **Known Facts** 1. Known as *the weeping prophet.* 2. Lived in Anathoth (Je.1:1; 29:27). 3. Was the son of Hilkiah (Je.1:1). 4. Served as a priest in the line of Abiathar. 5. Called as a youth. 6. Is thought to have written a large portion of the Bible: *1 & 2 Kings, Jeremiah, Lamentations.* **Predictions and Messages** 1. The vision of the almond branch (Je. 1:11-12). 2. The vision of the steaming pot (Je. 1:13-16). 3. The sermon about Israel's disobedience to God's Word and the coming judgment (Je. 2:1-6; 34:17; 35:17). 4. The sermon that Judah will be taken captive if they do not repent (Je.7:1-7; 26:1-7). 5. The prophecy that the house of the LORD will be made into a den of robbers (Je. 7:11; Mt.21:13). 6. The lesson of the linen waistband (Je. 13:1-10). 7. The prophecy of a great drought (Je.14:1-7). 8. The illustration of no comfort based upon the fact that Jeremiah remained unmarried (Je.16:1-6). 9. The sermon about observing the Sabbath (Je.17:20-27). 10. The illustration of the potter and the clay (Je.18:1-6). 11. The illustration of the broken jar (Je.19:1-6). 12. The sermon about administering righteous justice (Je.21:11-14). *(Cont. on next page)*	**Time** *627–562 B.C., after the fall of Samaria until long after the final captivity of Judah, from King Josiah to King Gedaliah.* **Place** *Jerusalem until he was forced to go to Egypt.*	Many important prophecies and messages have been given to the world by the LORD through His prophet Jeremiah: Often the LORD aroused Jeremiah to use symbols or illustrated sermons to demonstrate the message of his prophecy. Of all his prophecies (some foretelling, but most preaching), one overall message comes through loud and clear: The LORD will rise up. Over and over Jeremiah's messages pointed out that God arises in favor of those who truly serve Him, and in judgment of those who refuse to hear His Word. God will arise and defend His faithful followers, delivering them from evil circumstances. God will even change His mind about judging a person if that person truly repents and then follows the LORD completely, trusting fully in His power to save. **And though the LORD has sent all his servants the prophets to you again and again, you have not listened or paid any attention (Je.25:4).** **"O house of Israel, can I not do with you as this potter does?" declares the LORD. "Like clay in the hand of the potter, so are you in my hand, O house of Israel. If at any time I announce that a nation or kingdom is to be uprooted, torn down and destroyed, and if that nation I warned repents of its evil, then I will relent and not inflict on it the disaster I had planned. And if at another time I announce that a nation or kingdom is to be built up and planted, and if it does evil in my sight and does not obey me, then I will reconsider the good I had intended to do for it (Je.18:6-10).** **"Therefore, this is what the LORD God Almighty, the God of Israel, says: 'Listen! I am going to bring on Judah and on everyone living in Jerusalem every disaster I pronounced against them. I spoke to them, but they did not listen; I called to them, but they did not answer.'" Then Jeremiah said to the family of the Recabites, "This is what the LORD Almighty, the God of Israel, says: 'You have obeyed the command of your forefather Jonadab and have followed all**	God is not some far away Being Who has no interest in what happens in the world. The LORD is the Creator of the earth and everything and everyone in it. He created every person for the purpose of worshipping Him, that men and women might have communion, a personal relationship, with Him. He is zealous for the souls of people. He rises up, calling for people to turn from sin and follow Him. But God will not rise up in our behalf forever. Eventually the time of judgment comes. And when the instant comes for judgment, judgment will fall swiftly and justly. Every person will be placed on the scales of judgment. It is then that a person must be on the side of Jesus Christ, God's Son. Always remember this unchanging fact: Without being on Christ's side, the scales of judgment will never tip in our favor, no matter what: ➢ No matter how much money we have given to the church or charity. ➢ No matter how many people we have helped. ➢ No matter how *good* we have been. ➢ No matter how much we have sacrificed. ➢ No matter how we die, even if we paid the supreme sacrifice of dying as a martyr. The teaching of Scripture is definite. It is crystal clear. Even if a person were to give his life for another, it would not remove his sin nor make him acceptable to God. Christ is the only way to become acceptable to God. **For I take no pleasure in the death of anyone, declares the Sovereign LORD. Repent and live! (Eze.18:32).** **Salvation is found in no one else, for there is no other name under heaven given to men by which we must be saved" (Ac.4:12).**

PROPHET	TIME/PLACE GIVEN	MAIN MESSAGE	PRACTICAL APPLICATION
JEREMIAH (cont.) 13. The prophecy of the judgment against Jehoiachin (Je.22:29-30). 14. The prophecy that the righteous Messiah would be from the family line of King David (Je.23:5-6; 33:15). 15. The vision of the good and the bad figs (Je.24:1-10). 16. The prophecy that Judah will be taken to Babylon as captives (Je.25:8-9). 17. The sermon about the cup of God's wrath (Je.25:15-17). 18. The illustration of the yoke—a symbol of the power of Nebucadnazzar, king of Babylon, over other nations (Je.27:1-6). 19. The prediction that Hananiah, the false prophet, will die (Je.27:1-6). 20. The prediction of the public execution of the false prophets, Ahab and Zedekiah, by the hand of Nebuchadnezzar, the invading Babylonian king (Je.29:21-23). 21. The prediction of the destruction of the family of Shemaiah (Je.29:30). 22. The prophecy of promised restoration to Israel (Je.30:1-3; 31:10). 23. The prophecy of the slaughter of the infants in Bethlehem at the time of Christ (Je.31:15; Mt.2:17). 24. A prophecy of the new eternal covenant to be made with Israel (Je. 31:31-34; He. 8:8-12). 25. The prediction that King Zedekiah will die in captivity (Je. 34:4-5). 26. The prediction that Jehoiakim's family will all die (Je.36:30). **Scripture References** The book of *Jeremiah*; 2 Chr.35:25; 36:12, 21-22		his instructions and have done everything he ordered.' Therefore, this is what the LORD Almighty, the God of Israel, says: 'Jonadab son of Recab will never fail to have a man to serve me'"(Je.35:17-19).	

THE PROPHETS

PROPHET	TIME/PLACE GIVEN	MAIN MESSAGE	PRACTICAL APPLICATION
JESUS CHRIST (Jehovah is Salvation) **Known Facts** 1. Is God's Son, the King of kings and LORD of lords, the Messiah, the Savior of the world (Mt.14:33; Mk.1:1; Lu. 1:35; 1 Ti.6:15; Re. 17:14; 19:16). 2. Is proclaimed by the Scriptures from Genesis to Revelation. 3. Stands forever as Prophet, Priest, and King (De.18:18; He. 5:6; Re.19:16). 4. Is the subject of endless facts too numerous to mention. **Predictions and Messages** 1. The proclamation that God wants to save every person ever born in the world (Jn.3:16). 2. The prophecy that the people would ask for Him to perform miracles of healing (Lu. 4:23). 3. The declaration that anyone who does not follow His teaching will be destroyed (Mt. 7:24-27). 4. The prophecy of the destruction of Jerusalem in A.D. 70 (Mt. 24:2; Mk.13:2). 5. The prophecy that the end of the world would come and terrible judgment would fall (Mt.24:1–25:46). 6. The prediction that Peter would deny the LORD three times in one night (Mt.26:34; Mk.14:30; Lu.22:34; Jn.13:38). 7. The prophecy that Christ would be killed and rise again on the third day (Mt.12:40; 17:22-23; 20:18-19; Mk.8:31; 9:31; 10:33-34; Lu.18:32-33). (cont. in col. 3) **Scripture References** De.18:15-18; Mt.21:11; Lu.24:19; Ac.7:37	**Time** *During the years of Roman Oppression (A.D. 26-29) the Preeminent Prophet, the Son of God Himself was sent into the world in human flesh to save and set free all people of all generations.* **Place** *The nation of Israel under Roman rule.*	No greater prophet than Christ has ever lived—or ever will live—for no one else is perfect; no other prophet is God in the flesh. No greater message has ever been proclaimed—or ever will be—than the great gospel message, the good news of salvation. The good news is that Jesus Christ has come so that we can escape death and hell and have eternal life through Christ's death upon the cross and His resurrection from the grave. Through Him we will live with God in perfection forever and ever. What more can be said? **"For God so loved the world that he gave his one and only Son, that whoever believes in him shall not perish but have eternal life (Jn.3:16).** **Predictions and Messages** (cont. from col. 1) 8. The prophecy that Christ would ascend to the right hand of the Father in heaven (Jn.6:62; 14:2-3; 16:10). 9. The prophecy that Christ would come again to judge the world, rewarding the faithful and punishing the wicked (Mt.10:42; 16:27; 22:13; 25:21; Re.22:12). 10. The prophecy that the end of this age and world was coming, coming suddenly and unexpectedly (Mt.24:1–25:46).	God loves every man, not just the religious and the good. He does not love only the people who love Him. He loves everyone, even the un-lovely and the unloving, the un-believing and the obstinate, the selfish and the greedy, the spiteful and the vengeful. God wants man to know His love. He wants to reach everyone in the world with His love. So God demonstrated His love in the most perfect way possible: He sent His Son into the world to reveal the truth of life to man and to pay the penalty of sin for man, in "behalf of man." Through the death of His Son upon the cross, God poured out the very life blood of His Son for man. No greater love could ever be expressed; no greater act could ever be carried out to show the depth of perfect love. **"Come, all you who are thirsty, come to the waters; and you who have no money, come, buy and eat! Come, buy wine and milk without money and without cost (Is.55:1).** **The Lord is not slow in keeping his promise, as some understand slowness. He is patient with you, not wanting anyone to perish, but everyone to come to repentance (2 Pe.3:9).** **But God demonstrates his own love for us in this: While we were still sinners, Christ died for us (Ro.5:8).** **Unlike the other high priests, he does not need to offer sacrifices day after day, first for his own sins, and then for the sins of the people. He sacrificed for their sins once for all when he offered himself (He.7:27).**

PROPHET	TIME/PLACE GIVEN	MAIN MESSAGE	PRACTICAL APPLICATION
JOEL **(Yahweh is God)** **Known Facts** 1. Was the son of Pethuel (Joel 1:1). 2. Wrote the book of *Joel* (Joel 1:1). 3. Prophesied in Judah for a short time during the ministry of Elisha. **Predictions and Messages** 1. The prophecy of the coming devastating locust invasion (Joel 1:1–2:20). 2. The prophecy that restoration will come to Israel in abundance (Joel 2:21-27). 3. The prophecy of the Day of Pentecost (Joel 2:28-32; Ac.2:1-24). 4. The prophecy that a remnant will escape the coming judgment because they will call upon the LORD (Joel 2:32). 5. The prophecy of God's judgment against evil nations (Joel 3:1-19). 6. The prophecy of God's greatness and the truth that Jerusalem is protected by God (Joel 3:16-21). **Scripture References** The book of *Joel*; Ac.2:16	**Time** *830 B.C., during the ministry of Elisha and during the reign of Joash, king of Judah* **Place** *Jerusalem and Judah, the Southern Kingdom.*	Joel predicted several national disasters. In particular, Joel predicted that a locust invasion was going to wipe out the land, one that would be talked about for generations. The plague would be so terrible that no harvest would be left, none whatsoever. But Joel also prophesied that the Spirit of God would come in a special way and that there would be tremendous days of refreshing for those who stay true to the Lord. The message of Joel teaches that those who call upon the Lord will be saved. Judgment will come because of sin, but it will not last forever. Blessing and restoration will also be sent by God, but only for those who are called by God's name, only for those who truly acknowledge the Lord as the only true and living God. **And everyone who calls on the name of the LORD will be saved; for on Mount Zion and in Jerusalem there will be deliverance, as the LORD has said, among the survivors whom the LORD calls (Joel 2:32).**	Man is self-centered and rebellious toward God. He likes to feel independent. Consequently, man is dead to God and resistant to the pulling call and quickening power of God. Both God and man have a part in salvation. God calls. He attracts, draws, pulls, and tugs at the heart of man to come. But note: God will not call forever. When a man senses the call and pull of God, he must act then and there. He must believe and make the decision to follow Christ. **I will lift up the cup of salvation and call on the name of the LORD (Ps.116:13).** **For, "Everyone who calls on the name of the Lord will be saved." (Ro.10:13).** **This is the day the LORD has made; let us rejoice and be glad in it (Ps.118:24).** **For he says, "In the time of my favor I heard you, and in the day of salvation I helped you." I tell you, now is the time of God's favor, now is the day of salvation (2 Co.6:2).**

PROPHET	TIME/PLACE GIVEN	MAIN MESSAGE	PRACTICAL APPLICATION

JOHN THE APOSTLE (Jehovah/Yahweh has been gracious)
 	
Known Facts
1. Was the son of Zebedee, the brother of James (Mt.10:2).
2. Called away from the fishing trade to follow Christ (Mt.4:21).
3. Followed Christ closely.
4. Wrote the *Gospel of John,* the *Epistles of 1, 2, 3 John,* and the book of *Revelation.*
5. Was the only one of the twelve apostles not to be martyred, although an attempt was made against his life.
 	
Predictions and Messages
The book of *Revelation*
 	
Scripture References
The book of *John,* the *Epistles of 1, 2, 3 John,* and the book of *Revelation*
	Time
	A.D. 95, near the end of John's life.
	
	Place
	The island of Patmos, where John was exiled after a failed attempt to kill him by boiling him in oil.
		All prophecy points to this undeniable fact: Jesus Christ is the King of kings and LORD of lords. The book of *Revelation* shows Christ in all His glory and splendor. Christ is the Righteous Judge, the Righteous Lamb and the Righteous King. *Revelation* teaches us that to overcome the world, we must be fully committed to following Christ, the One Who has already overcome the world.
		    God's purpose in revealing to John the great revelation of Christ is to focus attention upon the Lamb, the Lord Jesus Christ Himself, and His ultimate triumph over the world and its ungodliness and evil.
		    God's purpose is to show the great redemption that He is preparing for all those who truly believe and follow His Son. God's purpose is to show man that he can be saved from the terrible things that are coming upon the earth.
		
		    The revelation of Jesus Christ, which God gave him to show his servants what must soon take place. He made it known by sending his angel to his servant John (Re.1:1).
		    "To the angel of the church in Ephesus write: These are the words of him who holds the seven stars in his right hand and walks among the seven golden lampstands (Re.2:1).
		    Then I heard every creature in heaven and on earth and under the earth and on the sea, and all that is in them, singing: "To him who sits on the throne and to the Lamb be praise and honor and glory and power, for ever and ever!" (Re.5:13).
		    For the great day of their wrath has come, and who can stand?" (Re.6:17).
		    For the testimony of Jesus is the spirit of prophecy" (Re.19:10).
		    On his robe and on his thigh he has this name written: KING OF KINGS AND LORD OF LORDS (Re.19:16).
			God has appointed a day to judge the world. The day of judgment is set, already determined. God demands that all men repent now, repent of their sin and idolatry, from the vain imaginations of the world. Every man has a *concept,* a thought about God. But we should *seek* and find the only living and true God as revealed in the Holy Bible. This we do by reading and obeying His Word. Every person is personally responsible for forsaking the idols of this world and for finding God. Man is now to repent.
			    God wants people to know that they can be saved while there is still time for them to repent. It is God's purpose to lead people to repentance and salvation, to lead them to the glorious inheritance of the great redemption that is to be given to all true followers of the Lord Jesus Christ.
			
			    O Jerusalem, wash the evil from your heart and be saved. How long will you harbor wicked thoughts? (Je.4:14).
			    In the past God overlooked such ignorance, but now he commands all people everywhere to repent (Ac.17:30).
			    By the same word the present heavens and earth are reserved for fire, being kept for the day of judgment and destruction of ungodly men (2 Pe.3:7).
			    Since you know that you will receive an inheritance from the Lord as a reward. It is the Lord Christ you are serving (Col.3:24).

PROPHET	TIME/PLACE GIVEN	MAIN MESSAGE	PRACTICAL APPLICATION
JOHN THE BAPTIST (Jehovah/Yahweh has been gracious) **Known Facts** 1. Was the son of Zacharias the priest and Elisabeth, and the first cousin of Jesus Christ (Lu.1:5-63). 2. Was the forerunner of Jesus Christ (Mal. 4:4-6; Mt.11:12-15; 17:10-13). 3. Lived and preached in the countryside and desert places of Palestine (Mt. 3:1-4). 3. Was jailed and beheaded by Herod (Mk.6:24-28). **Predictions and Messages** The unmistakable declaration that Jesus of Nazareth is the Christ, the sacrificial Lamb of God, Who would take away the sin of the world (Jn.1:29). **Scripture References** Mal.4:5; Mt.11:9; Mk.11:32; Lu.7:26; Jn.20:6	**Time** *A.D. 26, at the beginning of the earthly ministry of Jesus Christ.* **Place** *The Jordan River, about 20 miles east of Jerusalem.*	Jesus Christ is "the Lamb of God Who takes away the sin of the world" (Jn.1:29). Christ declared an astonishing thing: John the Baptist was the greatest man ever born of a woman. John was neither a prince nor a king. He was not a man of wealth, fame, or power. Who was he? Why would Christ make such a striking statement about him? He was simply a man who believed in the Messiah and who totally committed his life to that belief. But notice: John was chosen for this special task because he was so dedicated, so committed to God. John lived a life of total dedication to the Lord and of self-denial. He rejected the carnal, fleshly pleasures of this world and the coveting of its possessions. **The next day John saw Jesus coming toward him and said, "Look, the Lamb of God, who takes away the sin of the world! (Jn.1:29).**	God does not value a man by his social status nor by how far he gets in this world, but by his commitment to Jesus Christ. Christ declared John's eminence over all men; and in John, we have a blazing example of humility, of self-denial and commitment to God. And Christ declared that those who humble themselves will be greater still in the kingdom of God. It is an astonishing thought! But that is how much God values commitment and humility. **I tell you the truth: Among those born of women there has not risen anyone greater than John the Baptist; yet he who is least in the kingdom of heaven is greater than he (Mt.11:11).** **For this is what the high and lofty One says—he who lives forever, whose name is holy: "I live in a high and holy place, but also with him who is contrite and lowly in spirit, to revive the spirit of the lowly and to revive the heart of the contrite (Is.57:15).** **For whoever exalts himself will be humbled, and whoever humbles himself will be exalted (Mt.23:12).** **Humble yourselves before the Lord, and he will lift you up (Js.4:10).**

THE PROPHETS

PROPHET	TIME/PLACE GIVEN	MAIN MESSAGE	PRACTICAL APPLICATION
JONAH (Dove) **Known Facts** 1. Was the son of Ammitai (2 K.14:25; Jona.1:1). 2. Wrote the book of *Jonah* (Jona.1:1). 3. Ministered to the Northern Kingdom of Israel (2 K.14:25). 4. Tried to resist obeying God's instructions to go to Nineveh (Jona.1:3). 5. Was called to a foreign nation (Jona.1:2). 6. Converted the entire city of Nineveh with his preaching (Jona.3:5-10). 7. Lived in Gath-Hepher (2 K.14:25). 8. Quoted the Psalms repeatedly in his prayer for God to save him from the great fish (Jona.2:2-9) **Predictions and Messages** 1. Nineveh will be over-thrown in forty days (Jona.3:4). 2. Israel's borders will be extended and restored to their original positions (2 K.14:25). **Scripture References** The book of *Jonah*; 2 K.14:25; Mt.12:39-41; 16:4	**Time** *780–765 B.C., during the reign of Jeroboam II, king of Israel.* **Place** *Nineveh, the capital of Assyria, about 500 miles east of Israel.*	Jonah was called by God to preach to Nineveh, the capital city of the Assyrians. But Jonah did not want to go. He had a simple reason: The Assyrians were known for their cruelty to his people. Their war strategy was not only designed to take control of lands, but to instill absolute terror in the people they were conquering. The Assyrians wanted to make sure that the people would be so afraid of them that they would not ever try to avoid paying the demanded tribute each year. So Jonah tried to run away from God. Jonah got on a ship sailing in the opposite direction. But God sent a storm. Jonah knew why the storm had come. At Jonah's request, the men of the ship threw him overboard. But God was gracious. He had a great fish prepared to swallow Jonah. When Jonah repented, the fish threw Jonah up onto the land. After recovering from his ordeal, the repentant prophet went to Nineveh and preached. The city repented too, and they were saved from judgment. The book of *Jonah* clearly teaches that no matter how evil a person is, God will forgive him if he truly repents. No place represented self-exaltation and opposition to God more than Nineveh. God was so angry with the Ninevites that their total destruction was only forty days away. Yet, when they repented, God relented, forgave Nineveh and spared the city. **But I, with a song of thanksgiving, will sacrifice to you. What I have vowed I will make good. Salvation comes from the LORD" (Jona.2:9).** **But let man and beast be covered with sackcloth. Let everyone call urgently on God. Let them give up their evil ways and their violence. Who knows? God may yet relent and with compassion turn from his fierce anger so that we will not perish." When God saw what they did and how they turned from their evil ways, he had compassion and did not bring upon them the destruction he had threatened (Jona.3:8-10).**	We can now obtain the mercy of God. We need God to have mercy upon us because we have sinned against Him. We have done everything imaginable against God... • ignored Him • neglected Him • rebelled against Him • disobeyed Him • rejected Him • denied Him • cursed Him God will forgive our sins; He will have mercy upon us. But we must come to the throne of grace and ask for mercy. We must humble ourselves and fully acknowledge that mercy comes only through Christ Jesus. **Who is a God like you, who pardons sin and forgives the transgression of the remnant of his inheritance? You do not stay angry forever but delight to show mercy (Mi.7:18).**

THE PROPHETS

PROPHET	TIME/PLACE GIVEN	MAIN MESSAGE	PRACTICAL APPLICATION
JOSEPH **(He has added)** **Known Facts** 1. Was the son of Jacob (Ge.29:22-24). 2. Was persecuted and sold into slavery by his brothers (Ge. 37:4; 23-28). 3. Was forced to live in Egypt, a slave to Potiphar, falsely accused by his master's wife (Ec.39:1-2; 11-17). 4. Remained faithful to God (Ec.39:21-23). 5. Raised up after many years in prison to the throne of Egypt, second only to Pharaoh (Ge. 41:39-41). 6. Had a gift from God for interpreting dreams (Ge.40:6-22). **Predictions and Messages** 1. Pharaoh's butler would be restored to his position (Ge. 40:9-13). 2. Pharaoh's baker would be executed (Ge. 40:16-19). 3. Seven years of bountiful harvest would come to Egypt, but they would be followed by seven years of terrible famine (Ge.41:25-32). **Scripture References** Ge.40:1-23; 41:1-32	**Time** *1900–1885 B.C., during Joseph's reign as secondary only to Pharaoh of Egypt.* **Place** *Ancient Egypt, during the time of the Pharaohs.*	God is in complete control, and He carries out His plan regardless of the evil intentions of mankind. Joseph had all kinds of evil done against him. He was... • hated and persecuted by his brothers • sold into slavery • reported dead to his father • tempted by an immoral woman • falsely accused of adultery • imprisoned for twenty years Despite all of these awful experiences, God's purpose for Joseph was not stopped, not even hindered. At just the right time, God lifted Joseph up to be the second highest ranking official in Egypt, second only to Pharaoh himself. Even then Joseph did not take credit for himself. He gave all honor and praise to God for the interpretation of the dreams of Pharaoh. Through dreams, God delivered Joseph out of all his troubles and used him in a mighty way to save lives of multiplied thousands. **Within three days Pharaoh will lift up your head and restore you to your position, and you will put Pharaoh's cup in his hand, just as you used to do when you were his cupbearer (Ge.40:13).** **Within three days Pharaoh will lift off your head and hang you on a tree. And the birds will eat away your flesh" (Ge.40:19).** **Seven years of great abundance are coming throughout the land of Egypt, but seven years of famine will follow them. Then all the abundance in Egypt will be forgotten, and the famine will ravage the land (Ge.41:29-30).** **The reason the dream was given to Pharaoh in two forms is that the matter has been firmly decided by God, and God will do it soon (Ge.41:32).** **You intended to harm me, but God intended it for good to accomplish what is now being done, the saving of many lives (Ge.50:20).**	God's plans overrule man's opposition. God's counsel controls the evil of men, subjecting and using even the wickedness of men to work all things out for good and to achieve His will for the earth. Not even rulers, no matter how powerful they are, can stop or hinder the hand of God. People do all kinds of evil, trying to control situations, trying to rule over someone or to exert some authority beyond their position. Just think for a moment of the terrible evil things people in the world do every day. They ... • hate • steal • murder • destroy • commit immorality • encourage others to sin • revile those who will not take part in their sin • persecute believers • even attempt to stamp out the gospel and the church But no matter what people do, they cannot stop the will of God and His plan. They will fail, for God has a plan and He will overrule and carry out His plan. Kings and rulers stand up and rally against God and His Christ, the Messiah. They stand against, stand in opposition to and in hostility toward Christ, foolishly thinking that they always have and always will over-throw God's plan. But they will fail. God's great plan of salvation will continue to march triumphantly down through the ages of history. Despite the railings of the devil and all his forces, God's church will go forward, will grow and conquer more and more. God rules and will continue to rule over all the evil plans of men. It is critical to know that God not only has a plan for the world, but for every person. The believer can rest assured that nothing can stop the plan God has for his life. **The LORD foils the plans of the nations; he thwarts the purposes of the peoples. But the plans of the LORD stand firm forever, the purposes of his heart through all generations (Ps.33:10-11).** **Consider what God has done: Who can straighten what he has made crooked? (Ec.7:13).**

THE PROPHETS

PROPHET	TIME/PLACE GIVEN	MAIN MESSAGE	PRACTICAL APPLICATION
MALACHI (My messenger) **Known Facts** 1. Prophesied after the captivity in Judah. 2. Lived in the time of Nehemiah. 3. Was the last of the Old Testament writers. **Predictions and Messages** 1. The declaration that God has always loved Israel (Mal. 1:1-5). 2. The declaration that worship must be sincere (Mal.1:6-14). 3. The declaration that failing to honor the LORD results in a curse (Mal.2:1-9). 4. The declaration that marriage is holy before the LORD (Mal. 2:10-16). 5. The call to return to the LORD (Mal.2:17–3:7). 6. The declaration that a person must not rob God of His tithes and offering, not if the person wishes to be blessed by God. (Mal. 3:8-12). 7. The prophecy concerning the judgment of the wicked—they will not be spared (Mal.3:13-18). 8. The declaration that the righteous will triumph (Mal.4:1-3). 9. The prophecy that one like Elijah (John the Baptist) will come as a forerunner to the Messiah (Mal.4:4-6; Mt. 11:12-15; 17:10-13). **Scripture References** The book of *Malachi*	**Time** *430 B.C., about one hundred years after the Temple had been rebuilt under the direction of Haggai and Zechariah. Malachi was the last of the prophets to appear until Christ was born.* **Place** *Jerusalem, the capital city of the Southern Kingdom of Judah.*	Many of Malachi's listeners had participated in the great revivals of Ezra and Nehemiah and had fully committed their lives to the LORD. But now, just a few years later, they had slipped away from the LORD, turning back to a life of sin and neglecting the worship of the LORD and their duty to support the House of God (1:6-14; 3:6-12). The people were apathetic, complacent, only half-heartedly committed to the LORD. They needed to be called back to God. Thus God raised up Malachi to preach the utter necessity of repentance. In scathing sermon after scathing sermon, he pointed out the seriousness of Israel's sin. He called the people to return to the true worship of God. **My name will be great among the nations, from the rising to the setting of the sun. In every place incense and pure offerings will be brought to my name, because my name will be great among the nations," says the LORD Almighty (Mal.1:11).** **Ever since the time of your forefathers you have turned away from my decrees and have not kept them. Return to me, and I will return to you," says the LORD Almighty. "But you ask, 'How are we to return?' (Mal.3:7).**	True worship means more than ceremony, ritual and form. True worship must be sincere in heart, completely genuine. True worship, worship which truly draws us closer to the LORD must be five things: ➢ Worshipping the only living and true God, the worship of Him and Him alone. ➢ Approaching and seeking God's acceptance exactly as He says through the substitute sacrifice of the Lord Jesus Christ. ➢ Living for God by following the Lord Jesus Christ and obeying His holy Word. ➢ Hoping in the resurrection and not holding on to this world, but looking to the next. ➢ Always seeking to have a pure conscience. This means… • struggling, even to the point of pain, to keep a pure conscience • struggling to be *void of offense*—to keep from stumbling and from causing others to stumble • struggling to have a clear conscience toward both God and men **You shall have no foreign god among you; you shall not bow down to an alien god (Ps.81:9).** **Yet a time is coming and has now come when the true worshipers will worship the Father in spirit and truth, for they are the kind of worshipers the Father seeks (Jn.4:23).** **So that you may be able to discern what is best and may be pure and blameless until the day of Christ (Ph.1:10).**

THE PROPHETS

PROPHET	TIME/PLACE GIVEN	MAIN MESSAGE	PRACTICAL APPLICATION
MICAH (Who Is Like Jehovah/Yahweh?) **Known Facts** 1. Lived in Moresheth (Mi.1:1). 2. Wrote the book of *Micah* (Mi.1:1). 3. Ministered only a few years, but prophesied to both the Northern and Southern Kingdom (Mi.1:1). 4. Prophesied with Isaiah (Mi.1:1; Je.26:18; see Is.36-39). **Predictions and Messages** 1. The prophecy of God's judgment against Samaria and Jerusalem for idolatry (Mi.1). 2. The prophecy that judgment will come against social injustice (Mi.2:1-11). 3. The prophecy that there will be restoration for those remaining (Mi.2:12-13). 4. The prophecy that wicked leaders will be judged (Mi.3). 5. The prophecy of the promise of peace and purity of worship (Mi.4:1-5). 6. The prophecy that Israel will be made strong (Mi.4:6–5:1). 7. The prophecy that Christ will be born in Bethlehem (Mi.5:2-6; Mt.2:5-6). 8. The prophecy that Israel will be pure from the idolatry of the world (Mi.5:7-15). 9. A sermon about what God requires of a person (Mi.6). 10. A sermon concerning the terrible corruption among the people (Mi.7:1-6). 11. A prayer of repentance (Mi.7:7-11). 12. The prophecy about Israel's future restoration (Mi.7:12-20). **Scripture References** The book of *Micah*; Je.26:18; Mt. 2:5-6	**Time** *735–725 B.C., during the reigns of Jotham, Ahaz, and Hezekiah.* **Place** *Judea, Jerusalem, and Samaria.*	In Micah's day, the Assyrians were just a few years away (722 B.C.) from conquering Samaria, the capital of the Northern Kingdom of Israel. The Assyrians would be within easy striking distance of Jerusalem. Although Micah sternly warned Judah that a terrible situation was coming for the nation, the religious leaders would not believe it. Micah preached that not even God's holy mountain would be spared. But the leaders assumed that since the temple and God's Holy Place was in Jerusalem, the foreign invasion was impossible. Their pride would lead to their downfall. Micah warned the people: The LORD absolutely requires justice, mercy and humility. No matter how much we do in the name of the LORD, without these three things, we cannot hope to be acceptable before God. Without living the way God requires, judgment will come, terrible judgment. But if we walk humbly before people, showing mercy and executing justice, and truly worshipping the LORD, the LORD will accept us. For He accepts all who obey His Word and walk humbly before Him. **With what shall I come before the LORD and bow down before the exalted God? Shall I come before him with burnt offerings, with calves a year old? Will the LORD be pleased with thousands of rams, with ten thousand rivers of oil? Shall I offer my firstborn for my transgression, the fruit of my body for the sin of my soul? He has showed you, O man, what is good. And what does the LORD require of you? To act justly and to love mercy and to walk humbly with your God. Listen! The LORD is calling to the city— and to fear your name is wisdom—"Heed the rod and the One who appointed it (Mi.6:6-9).**	God is to be feared, for He resists and stands opposed to the proud. The very thing we do not want to be is prideful. For the only way to escape the judgment of God's hand is to humble ourselves under His mighty hand. If we stand up to His hand, we will be stricken down; but if we humble ourselves under His hand, we will be protected and lifted up, exalted forever and ever. God is going to exalt the humble. The day is coming when the humble will be exalted in all the glory and majesty of Christ. They will be exalted to live with Christ, ruling and reigning with Him and serving Him throughout the entire universe. They will be with Christ, worshipping and serving Him forever and ever. **Humble yourselves, therefore, under God's mighty hand, that he may lift you up in due time (1 Pe.5:6).** **Humble yourselves before the Lord, and he will lift you up (Js.4:10).** **But you, O God, will bring down the wicked into the pit of corruption; bloodthirsty and deceitful men will not live out half their days. But as for me, I trust in you (Ps.55:23).**

THE PROPHETS

PROPHET	TIME/PLACE GIVEN	MAIN MESSAGE	PRACTICAL APPLICATION
MICAIAH (Who is like Jehovah/Yahweh?) **Known Facts** 1. Was the son of Imlah (1 K.22:8-9). 2. Suffered persecution for speaking the Word of the LORD (1 K. 22:24). **Predictions and Messages** 1. The prophecy that King Ahab of Israel and King Jehoshaphat of Judah would meet with disaster if they tried to battle the Aramean (Syrian) army (2 Chr.18:16). 2. The declaration that the LORD had allowed a lying spirit to influence the false prophets so that Ahab would be enticed into battle and to his doom (1 K.22:19-23; 2 Chr. 18:18-22). **Scripture References** 1 K.22:1-37; 2 Chr.18:1-34	**Time** *853 B.C., at the end of the reign of King Ahab.* **Place** *Samaria, the capital of the Northern Kingdom.*	The battle at Ramoth-Gilead would be a disaster. Micaiah gave this prophetic message to King Ahab of Israel and King Jehoshaphat of Judah, who were planning to attack the Arameans (Syrians). Even though an attendant of the king warned Micaiah not to give a negative message to King Ahab, he advised that everyone go home and not fight the Arameans (Syrians) at this time. But the LORD had allowed a lying spirit to influence the false prophets to speak in unison so that Ahab would go against what the LORD had truly said. Because of his terribly wicked life and rule, God's longsuffering with Ahab had run its course. Now, it was time for Ahab to face the judgment of God. **Then Micaiah answered, "I saw all Israel scattered on the hills like sheep without a shepherd, and the LORD said, 'These people have no master. Let each one go home in peace'" (2 Chr.18:16).** **"So now the LORD has put a lying spirit in the mouths of all these prophets of yours. The LORD has decreed disaster for you" (1 K.22:23).**	We must guard ourselves against false prophets and false teachers, for the world is full of both. Far too often, the pulpits of the world are filled with false prophets who preach a doctrine other than the doctrine of Christ and His Holy Word. Their focus is not the Word of God but some other religious literature or some feel-good message. Ignoring the truth of God's Word, they seek the approval of their congregations by tickling their ears with messages of positive thinking and self-esteem or by placing too much emphasis on healing and miracles or a particular spiritual gift. These subjects are important, for they are each a part of God's Word. But the whole counsel of God's Word is to be proclaimed—both negative and positive. False prophets seek merely to captivate or pacify us, giving us messages they feel will secure our approval and enhance their own honor and recognition. We must guard against false teachers, wherever they come from, whatever position they have. False teachers mislead us into half-truths, lies and serious doctrinal error, which will lead to destruction. **"Watch out for false prophets. They come to you in sheep's clothing, but inwardly they are ferocious wolves (Mt.7:15).**

Body.

THE PROPHETS

PROPHET	TIME/PLACE GIVEN	MAIN MESSAGE	PRACTICAL APPLICATION
MOSES (Drawn out) **Known Facts** 1. Was the only prophet of Old Testament times with whom God spoke face-to-face (Ex.33:11). 2. Was born into the tribe of Levi (Ex. 6:16-20). 3. Was the son of Amram and Jochebed (Ex.6:20). 4. Was raised as an Egyptian (Ex.2:1-10; He.11:26-27). 5. Ran from Egypt to escape from a murder charge (Ex.2:11-15). 6. Heard God speak from the burning bush where God revealed His Name to him (Ex.3:1-14). 7. Led the people of Israel out of bondage (Ex.14:21-31). 8. Performed many miraculous signs (Ex. 4:30; 7:20; 8:6, 17; 9:10, 23; 10:13, 22; 14:21, 27). 9. Received the Law from God on Mt. Sinai (Ex.19:1–24:18). 10. Received the instructions for the Tabernacle from God on Mt. Sinai (Ex.25:1–31:18). 11. Was prevented from entering the promised land because he disobeyed God (De.34:4). 12. Wrote the Pentateuch, the first five books of the Bible. **Predictions and Messages** 1. The prophecy of the coming Messiah, the Savior of the world (De.18:15-18). 2. The Song of Moses: a prophecy concerning the future of Israel (De.32:1-43). 3. The Blessing of Moses: a prophecy concerning the future of each of the twelve tribes of Israel (De.33:1-29). (cont. on next page)	**Time** *1405 B.C., near the end of Moses' life.* **Place** *Across the Jordan from the promised land, in the Arabah, the dry desert land east of the Jordan River.*	Throughout his final forty years, Moses proclaimed the holiness and sovereignty of the LORD. During this time of leading the Israelites in the exodus from Egypt to the promised land of blessing, Moses wrote the first five books of the Bible (which is really one great book called *the Law* or *the Instruction* or *the Pentateuch*). In these Scriptures are found: 1. The beginnings of the world and the Israelite nation (*Genesis*). 2. The account of Israel's Exodus from Egypt, their escape from bondage: A type of escaping from the bondage of sin (*Exodus*). 3. The Law of God which Moses received on Mt. Sinai (*Exodus*). 4. The instructions for the Tabernacle, the place of worship: A picture of heaven (*Exodus*). 5. The instructions for the sacrifices, showing how man can approach God and be acceptable to God: The sacrifices foreshadowed Jesus Christ and His sacrifice as a sin offering. Through His sacrifice a person can be saved from sin, death and hell (*Leviticus*). 6. The journeys of the Israelite people: powerful lessons on following God (*Numbers*). 7. The sermons of Moses: the first studies concerning the nature and character of God and how people can follow and live for God (*Deuteronomy*). Thus the Mosaic Covenant, the law of God, lays the groundwork for all that follows in the Old Testament and in the Bible. For the Law points out that we need a Savior and that we must humbly come to God on His terms, offering the Sacrifice that He demands. The Law also points out that the believer must be separated from the world, refusing to live like the world and not being conformed to the world. The Law of Moses proclaims the very same message the entire Bible proclaims, that we need the salvation provided in Jesus Christ, God's Son. Moses preached his series of sermons (found in the book of *Deuteronomy*) as the children of Israel were getting ready to enter the promise Land. At the end of his life, he warned Israel not to forget the LORD, not to go astray as they had in the past.	The greatest commandment is clear: we must love God with all our heart, soul and strength. We must know that "the LORD our God is one LORD" (De.6:4). Note these three vital facts about this great declaration: ➤ God is the *only* living and true God, the only God Who can save, deliver and redeem. ➤ The Lord is our God. We have a personal relationship with the Lord. It is a daily experience. We are His people, the sheep of His pasture. Therefore, we should love, adore and worship Him. ➤ The Lord is one Lord. There is no other. The many false gods of the world exist only in the imaginations of people. Look at how great God is! No wonder the Scripture commands us to love God with our whole being, with all of our heart, soul, mind and strength. We are to love Him thoroughly, fully, completely—in every way for the rest of our lives. **He said to them, "Take to heart all the words I have solemnly declared to you this day, so that you may command your children to obey carefully all the words of this law. They are not just idle words for you—they are your life. By them you will live long in the land you are crossing the Jordan to possess" (De.32:46-47).** **For the law was given through Moses; grace and truth came through Jesus Christ (Jn.1:17).** **Hear, O Israel: The LORD our God, the LORD is one. Love the LORD your God with all your heart and with all your soul and with all your strength (De.6:4-5).**

PROPHET	TIME/PLACE GIVEN	MAIN MESSAGE	PRACTICAL APPLICATION
MOSES (cont.) **Scripture References** The books of *Genesis, Exodus, Leviticus, Numbers,* and *Deuteronomy*; Jos.8:31-32; 1 S.12:8; 1 K.8:56; 2 K.23:23-25; 1 Chr.22:13; Ps.90; Is.63:11-12; Mt.17:1-3		As he preached, Moses also broke out into song and prophesied of the future of Israel. Most importantly, Moses told of One Who would rise later, One Who would be similar to Moses. Moses spoke of the Messiah, Jesus Christ. Just as Moses spoke the words God gave him to speak so Jesus Christ spoke and did what the Father spoke and directed Him to do. Just as Moses delivered God's people from the bondage of Egypt so Christ delivers God's people from the bondage of sin. **The LORD your God will raise up for you a prophet like me from among your own brothers. You must listen to him....I will raise up for them a prophet like you from among their brothers; I will put my words in his mouth, and he will tell them everything I command him (De.18:15, 18).** **Listen, O heavens, and I will speak; hear, O earth, the words of my mouth. Let my teaching fall like rain and my words descend like dew, like showers on new grass, like abundant rain on tender plants. I will proclaim the name of the LORD. Oh, praise the greatness of our God! (De.32:1-3).** **This is the blessing that Moses the man of God pronounced on the Israelites before his death. He said: "The LORD came from Sinai and dawned over them from Seir; he shone forth from Mount Paran. He came with myriads of holy ones from the south, from his mountain slopes. Surely it is you who love the people; all the holy ones are in your hand. At your feet they all bow down, and from you receive instruction (De.33:1-3).**	

PROPHET	TIME/PLACE GIVEN	MAIN MESSAGE	PRACTICAL APPLICATION
NAHUM (Comfort) **Known Facts** 1. Lived in Elkosh (Na. 1:1). 2. Prophesied about Nineveh, just as Jonah did, but the Ninevites did not listen to Nahum, and they were destroyed (Na.2:8-13). 3. Wrote the book of *Nahum* (Na.1:1). **Predictions and Messages** 1. A poem about God's zeal for justice—His goodness and protection for those who take refuge in Him and His fierce wrath that falls upon the wicked (Na.1:2-8). 2. The doom of the Ninevites, who will be destroyed even though they have many weapons (Na.1:9-2:13). 3. A funeral poem about Nineveh, the greedy and violently wicked city (Na.3:1-19). **Scripture References** The book of *Nahum*; Is.52:7	**Time** *663–612 B.C., during the reign of Manasseh, Amon and Josiah.* **Place** *Judah, the Southern Kingdom and Nineveh, the capital city of Assyria, hundreds of miles from Jerusalem.*	The outcry of evil from Nineveh, the capital city of the Assyrians, reached up to God, calling out for judgment. And swift judgment was on the way. The Ninevites thought that they were unstoppable, too mighty to even be slowed down. For the small country of Judah, Nineveh personified the word terror. But Nahum had a message from God: the LORD is zealous, avenging His people and pouring out wrath upon His enemies. About one hundred years earlier, Nineveh had repented under conviction of Jonah's preaching to them. But now, the city had returned to its wicked and brutal ways, caring only about conquest and plunder, power and wealth. Nahum preached a message of total destruction. This time, the Ninevites did not repent and the judgment of God fell on the entire city. Tragically, the Ninevites had felt all powerful, so powerful that nothing or no one could harm their large fortified city. But when God pronounced judgment on them, nothing and no one could save them. Nineveh was destroyed in 663 B.C. **The LORD is a jealous and avenging God; the LORD takes vengeance and is filled with wrath. The LORD takes vengeance on his foes and maintains his wrath against his enemies. The LORD is slow to anger and great in power; the LORD will not leave the guilty unpunished. His way is in the whirlwind and the storm, and clouds are the dust of his feet (Na.1:2-3).** **Nothing can heal your wound; your injury is fatal. Everyone who hears the news about you claps his hands at your fall, for who has not felt your endless cruelty? (Na.3:19).**	God is going to rectify all the injustices of the world. God's judgment is going to fall upon every person who has mistreated others. All unjust behavior of men will bear the terrible judgment of God, all the... • killing • stealing • mocking • fighting • cursing • prejudice • cheating • bitterness • abusing • hatred The list could go on and on, but the point is this: much of the world's behavior is evil and unjust. God *must judge* the world, for judgment is the righteous and just penalty for evil. All the injustices of the world must be corrected. God is going to judge the world. He is just and righteous Himself; therefore, His very nature demands that all the injustices and wrongs that men have inflicted upon others be judged and punished. God will execute justice and avenge His people. God sees the great need of His people, and God alone can meet their need. Therefore God, the just Judge of the universe, will avenge them of their adversaries (spiritual as well as human). Even now, when His people pray, continually bringing their case before God, He hears their plea, and He delivers them. And when the time comes, justice will be executed against the persecutors of His people. **Will not the Judge of all the earth do right?" (Ge.18:25).** **And will not God bring about justice for his chosen ones, who cry out to him day and night? Will he keep putting them off? I tell you, he will see that they get justice, and quickly (Lu.18:7-8).** **Then men will say, "Surely the righteous still are rewarded; surely there is a God who judges the earth" (Ps.58:11).**

PROPHET	TIME/PLACE GIVEN	MAIN MESSAGE	PRACTICAL APPLICATION
NATHAN (He has given) **Known Facts** 1. Ministered during the time of the united kingdom under King David and King Solomon (2 S.7:1-5; 1 Chr. 17:1-4). 2. Named David's son Jedidiah (who later became known as Solomon) (2 S.12:25). 3. Stood with David against Adonijah the rebel, helping establish Solomon on the throne (1 K.1:8-46). 4. Wrote the history of the kingship of David and Solomon (1 Chr. 9:29; 2 Chr. 29:25). **Predictions and Messages** 1. The prophecy that Israel would have a permanent dwelling place (2 S.7:4-10; 1 Chr.17:3-9). 2. The prophecy that God would establish David's family on the throne forever—that the Messiah, the King of kings, would come through David's family (2 S.7:11-17; 1 Chr.17:10-15). 3. The parable of the poor sheep owner—the exposure of David's sin of adultery (2 S.12:1-9; Ps.51:1). 4. The prophecy that David's household would be filled with death and violence (2 S.12:10). 5. The prophecy that David's secret sin of adultery would be punished by a public sin of adultery against him (2 S.12:11-12). (Cont. on next page)	**Time** *1003-931 B.C., during the reigns of King David and King Solomon when the kingdom of Israel was still united and strong.* **Place** *Jerusalem, the capital of Israel and the city chosen by God to place the temple.*	Through all the messages sent by God through Nathan the prophet, this one theme stands out: the LORD will greatly bless and defend all who honor Him. King David had a burning desire to build a temple for the LORD. Nathan had encouraged David to build the temple; but that very night God corrected Nathan, reversing his counsel to David. Nonetheless, God was very pleased with David and blessed David greatly because David honored Him with his whole heart. Note the tremendous blessings that Nathan predicted would be given to David by God: ➢ David would be given a position of astounding royalty and power. ➢ David would have the blessing of God's presence and guidance through the years. ➢ David would be given the power to conquer his enemies. ➢ David would be given an honorable name and reputation. ➢ David was assured that the promised land would be given to Israel. ➢ David was assured that he would receive future rest from all his enemies. ➢ David would receive a never ending dynasty. ➢ David would receive a Promise Seed raised up by God Himself. ➢ David would receive a kingdom established by God Himself. ➢ David was given the promise that the temple would be built by his son. ➢ David was given the promise of a descendant Who would be God's own Son. ➢ David was given the promise that the same descendant would be punished for sin. Although David did not build the temple, he honored God by his burning desire to build it. God greatly blessed David because he had a heart that longed to give honor to God.	God is good, and His goodness is overwhelming. But we live in a wicked world, a world where evil men roam and commit acts of terror, violence and lawlessness. In addition to evil men, the world is full of misfortune and hardship, temptation and trial. Yet in the midst of all the difficulties and problems of life, God's goodness shines through. For if we trust the Lord, He promises to save and deliver us and to meet our every need. No matter what the terrible circum-stance, God will pour out His goodness upon us, strengthening and helping us to walk through any problem or difficulty. God is good, and He longs for us to trust Him. And if we trust Him, His goodness pours out the riches promises to us, promises that assure us of the most victorious and fruitful life imaginable. This is the wonderful promise of the incredible goodness of God. **"Why do you ask me about what is good?" Jesus replied. "There is only One who is good. If you want to enter life, obey the commandments" (Mt. 19:17).** **The LORD is my strength and my shield; my heart trusts in him, and I am helped. My heart leaps for joy and I will give thanks to him in song (Ps.28:7).** **You are good, and what you do is good; teach me your decrees (Ps.119:68).** **The LORD is good, a refuge in times of trouble. He cares for those who trust in him (Na.1:7).**

PROPHET	TIME/PLACE GIVEN	MAIN MESSAGE	PRACTICAL APPLICATION
NATHAN (cont.) 6. The declaration that God had seen David's repentance and had forgiven him of his adultery (2 S.12:13). 7. The prophecy that David and Bathsheba's son, born from their adulterous relationship, would die (2 S. 12:14). **Scripture References** 2 S.7:1-17; 1 K.1; 1 Chr.17		That night the word of the LORD came to Nathan, saying: "Go and tell my servant David, 'This is what the LORD says: Are you the one to build me a house to dwell in? I have not dwelt in a house from the day I brought the Israelites up out of Egypt to this day. I have been moving from place to place with a tent as my dwelling. Wherever I have moved with all the Israelites, did I ever say to any of their rulers whom I commanded to shepherd my people Israel, "Why have you not built me a house of cedar?"' "Now then, tell my servant David, 'This is what the LORD Almighty says: I took you from the pasture and from following the flock to be ruler over my people Israel. I have been with you wherever you have gone, and I have cut off all your enemies from before you. Now I will make your name great, like the names of the greatest men of the earth. And I will provide a place for my people Israel and will plant them so that they can have a home of their own and no longer be disturbed. Wicked people will not oppress them anymore, as they did at the beginning and have done ever since the time I appointed leaders over my people Israel. I will also give you rest from all your enemies. "'The LORD declares to you that the LORD himself will establish a house for you: When your days are over and you rest with your fathers, I will raise up your offspring to succeed you, who will come from your own body, and I will establish his kingdom. He is the one who will build a house for my Name, and I will establish the throne of his kingdom forever. I will be his father, and he will be my son. When he does wrong, I will punish him with the rod of men, with floggings inflicted by men. But my love will never be taken away from him, as I took it away from Saul, whom I removed from before you. Your house and your kingdom will endure forever before me; your throne will be established forever.'" Nathan reported to David all the words of this entire revelation (2 S.7:4-17).	

PROPHET	TIME/PLACE GIVEN	MAIN MESSAGE	PRACTICAL APPLICATION
NOAH (Rest) **Known Facts** 1. Was the son of Lamech (Ge.5:28-29). 2. Found favor in the sight of God (Ge.6:5-8). 3. Was a righteous man (Ge.6:9). 4. Received instruction from God to build an ark to preserve his family and some of each living animal (Ge.6:13-21). 5. Entered into a covenant with God to be saved (Ge.6:18). 6. Built the ark (Ge. 6:22). 7. Called a preacher of righteousness by the Scripture (2 Pe.2:5). 8. Was saved by following God's instructions (Ge.7:1-24). **Predictions and Messages** 1. Preached righteousness to a wicked generation (2 Pe.2:5). 2. Prophesied about the future of his three sons and their descendants (Ge.9:25-27). **Scripture References** Ge.5–8	**Time** *Unknown, but at least seven generations after Adam.* **Place** *The center of civilization, before the tower of Babel.*	Noah was a preacher of righteousness, warning people that the judgment of God was coming upon the whole world. What did he preach? Simply what God had told him—there is a consequence for sin. God would eventually withdraw his Spirit: His Spirit would not always strive with man, not forever. If man did not repent, the consequences of his sin would come upon him. Through the preaching of Noah, the Spirit of God was doing just what He does with people today when they hear the Word of God preached and taught in the power of God. He was convicting them of sin and of coming judgment. But the people were resisting and quenching the convictions of the Spirit. They were not listening to the voice of God struggling within their hearts. They wanted to live like they wanted, to do their own thing. Consequently, God had no choice. God had to give man a final warning: if man did not repent, God would withdraw His Spirit and let judgment fall upon the ungodliness and unrighteousness of men. **Then the LORD said, "My Spirit will not contend with man forever, for he is mortal; his days will be a hundred and twenty years."...So the LORD said, "I will wipe mankind, whom I have created, from the face of the earth—men and animals, and creatures that move along the ground, and birds of the air—for I am grieved that I have made them" (Ge.6:3, 7).** **He said, "Cursed be Canaan! The lowest of slaves will he be to his brothers." He also said, "Blessed be the LORD, the God of Shem! May Canaan be the slave of Shem. May God extend the territory of Japheth; may Japheth live in the tents of Shem, and may Canaan be his slave" (Ge.9:25-27).** **If he did not spare the ancient world when he brought the flood on its ungodly people, but protected Noah, a preacher of righteousness, and seven others (2 Pe. 2:5).**	Judgment for sin is coming. Yet, people act as if the world will go on undisturbed. People act as if tomorrow will be just like today. The world continues in sin, foolishly rushing here and there, living as if there is no consequence for sin. Think how much our society is like the first society of earth. Think of the cult of beauty and sex, the power given to the immoral, the sin that runs wild all through society. But it will not continue forever. Just like Noah's day, eventually God will withdraw His Spirit and judgment will fall. The terrible wrath of God will be made known to the sinner, either when he dies, or when the judgment of God falls upon the entire world. A person simply cannot live an immoral and wicked life and hope that God will not notice. There are consequences for sin, serious consequences. **As it was in the days of Noah, so it will be at the coming of the Son of Man. For in the days before the flood, people were eating and drinking, marrying and giving in marriage, up to the day Noah entered the ark; and they knew nothing about what would happen until the flood came and took them all away. That is how it will be at the coming of the Son of Man (Mt.24:37-39).** **The acts of the sinful nature are obvious: sexual immorality, impurity and debauchery; idolatry and witchcraft; hatred, discord, jealousy, fits of rage, selfish ambition, dissensions, factions and envy; drunkenness, orgies, and the like. I warn you, as I did before, that those who live like this will not inherit the kingdom of God (Ga.5:19-21).**

THE PROPHETS

PROPHET	TIME/PLACE GIVEN	MAIN MESSAGE	PRACTICAL APPLICATION
OBADIAH (Servant of Jehovah/Yahweh) **Known Facts** 1. Wrote the book of *Obadiah* (Ob.1). 2. Ministered to Judah, the Southern Kingdom of Israel (Ob.16-17). **Predictions and Messages** 1. The prophecy of the doom of the nation of Edom (Ob.1-16). 2. The prophecy that Judah will overpower Edom, taking away Edom's territory and ending the evil nation's violence against Judah (Ob.17-21). **Scripture References** The book of *Obadiah*; 2 K.8:20-22; 2 Chr.21:8-20	**Time** *845 B.C., during the reign of King Jehoram of Judah.* **Place** *Judah, the Southern Kingdom of Israel.*	Edom will be overthrown because of her pride, a pride which led to a lifestyle of wickedness, and savage brutality, and violence against the Israelites down through the centuries. The Edomites were the descendants of Esau and were actually related to Judah. Because of their ancient relationship, the Edomites should have been good neighbors to Judah, but instead they were hostile, brutal and savage. Now, God would make them pay for their arrogance. Edom would suffer one invasion after the other over the next several centuries. Eventually, just as predicted, in the second century B.C., the Maccabees, who were Jewish zealots, finally conquered the Edomites and subjected them under the heel of Judah's authority. **The vision of Obadiah. This is what the Sovereign LORD says about Edom—We have heard a message from the LORD: An envoy was sent to the nations to say, "Rise, and let us go against her for battle" (Ob.1).** **Though you soar like the eagle and make your nest among the stars, from there I will bring you down," declares the LORD (Ob.4).** **You should not look down on your brother in the day of his misfortune, nor rejoice over the people of Judah in the day of their destruction, nor boast so much in the day of their trouble (Ob.12).** **"The day of the LORD is near for all nations. As you have done, it will be done to you; your deeds will return upon your own head (Ob.15).**	All boasting and arrogance, pride and conceit is wrong. It is wrong to elevate ourselves above others, to think that we are *better* or *higher* than anyone else. God will severely judge all pride. **Therefore pride is their necklace; they clothe themselves with violence (Ps.73:6).** **They will spread out their hands in it, as a swimmer spreads out his hands to swim. God will bring down their pride despite the cleverness of their hands (Is.25:11).**

PROPHET	TIME/PLACE GIVEN	MAIN MESSAGE	PRACTICAL APPLICATION
PAUL (Small, little) **Known Facts** 1. Lived in Tarsus (Ac. 9:11; 21:39). 2. Was an apostle "born out of due time" (1 Co.15:8). 3. Was originally named *Saul* (Ac.13:9). 4. Persecuted the Christians, fiercely persecuted them (Ac.8:1–9:2). 5. Was converted in a dramatic confrontation with Christ (Ac. 9:3-9). 6. Became just as zealous for Christ as he had been for Judaism (2 Co.12:15). 7. Made many missionary journeys, taking the gospel to the world (Ac.13:1–28:31). 8. Was taken prisoner by the Roman empire (Ac.21:11-13; 25:14). 9. Wrote much of the New Testament. 10. Was martyred for the cause of Christ (by Nero in A.D. 64, according to church history). **Predictions and Messages** 1. A prophecy given to Paul by an angel—that all on board the ship caught in a storm would live (Ac.27:12-26). 2. A prophecy that Christ will return to the earth (Ph.3:20; 1 Th. 4:16. 3. A prophecy that the world will become very evil in the last times, with some saints even falling away (2 Th.2:3; 2 Ti. 3:1-7). 4. A prophecy that the saints of God will be resurrected (1 Co. 15:50-57; Ph.3:21; 1 Th.4:13-18). (cont. on next page)	**Time** *A.D. 35–64, all the years of Paul's life after his conversion.* **Place** *Various churches, homes and prisons, north and east of the Mediterranean Sea.*	If the message of Paul can be summed up in a few words, it can only be done in his own words: **I am not ashamed of the gospel, because it is the power of God for the salvation of everyone who believes: first for the Jew, then for the Gentile. For in the gospel a righteousness from God is revealed, a righteousness that is by faith from first to last, just as it is written: "The righteous will live by faith" (Ro.1:16-17).** **Yet when I preach the gospel, I cannot boast, for I am compelled to preach. Woe to me if I do not preach the gospel! (1 Co.9:16).** What greater example could be set before us than the life of Paul, other than the life of Christ? The Apostle Paul was the apex of dedication and service, surpassed only by Christ Himself. Paul exhausted himself preaching and teaching the gospel, finally giving his life as a martyr. In all the preaching and prophecies of Paul, there was one clear point, one unmistakable focus: the gospel of Jesus Christ, the good news that Christ paid the price for sin on Calvary. Every person who accepts this, calling on the name of the Lord, can be saved from his sins. This person can become acceptable to God and be given a wonderful entrance into heaven, the place of eternal reward and receive the Spirit of God into his heart and life. With the presence of God's Spirit in his life, the believer has the power to live a conquering triumphant life through all the trials and temptations of life. No matter what the believer faces—even if it is the terrible evil of the last days—God empowers the believer to be "more than a conqueror" (Ro.8:37-39). Think, when the believer comes face-to-face with death, quicker than the eye can blink, the Lord transfers him to heaven, the place of eternal reward.	The hope of salvation—the forgiveness of sins, a victorious and conquering life and the gift of eternal life—all this has been entrusted into the hands of Paul and to all other believers. Note exactly what the Bible teaches: God's Word and the teaching of God's Word have been committed to men by the commandment of God. God's Word and the preaching of His Word are not an option. God commands that we take care of His Word, that we be good stewards of the truth of the gospel, that we preach and teach it to the whole world. **Therefore go and make disciples of all nations, baptizing them in the name of the Father and of the Son and of the Holy Spirit, and teaching them to obey everything I have commanded you. And surely I am with you always, to the very end of the age." (Mt.28:19-20).** **He said to them, "Go into all the world and preach the good news to all creation (Mk. 16:15).** **Again Jesus said, "Peace be with you! As the Father has sent me, I am sending you" (Jn.20:21).**

PROPHET	TIME/PLACE GIVEN	MAIN MESSAGE	PRACTICAL APPLICATION
PAUL (cont.) 5. A prophecy of the antichrist—that the man of sin will be revealed in the end time (2 Th.2:1-5). 6. A prophecy that Christ will receive those who are His into heaven and their eternal reward (1 Co.1:8). 7. A prophecy that death will be destroyed (1 Co.15:24-26). **Scripture References** Ac.8:1–28:31; the books of Romans, 1 & 2 Corinthians, Galatians, Ephesians, Philippians, Colossians, 1 & 2 Thessalonians, 1 & 2 Timothy, Titus, Philemon		No, in all these things we are more than conquerors through him who loved us. For I am convinced that neither death nor life, neither angels nor demons, neither the present nor the future, nor any powers, neither height nor depth, nor anything else in all creation, will be able to separate us from the love of God that is in Christ Jesus our Lord (Ro.8:37-39). The Lord will rescue me from every evil attack and will bring me safely to his heavenly kingdom. To him be glory for ever and ever. Amen (2 Ti.4:18).	

PROPHET	TIME/PLACE GIVEN	MAIN MESSAGE	PRACTICAL APPLICATION
SAMUEL **(God hears)** **Known Facts** 1. Dedicated to God from birth (1 S.1:11; 2:18). 2. Was favored highly with God and man (1 S.2:26). 3. Was given prophecies from God even as a boy (1 S.3:1-18). 4. Was recognized as a prophet to all Israel (1 S.3:20). 5. Lived in Ramah (1 S. 7:17). 6. Appointed his sons as judges, but they were wicked (1 S.8:3). 7. Anointed Saul as king (1 S.10:1). 8. Recorded events of David's reign and the regulations to govern the king and control his power (1 S.10:25; 1 Chr.29:29). 9. Faithfully served as a judge all his days (1 S.12:1-5). 10. Called down rain and thunder during the dry season—a sign that Samuel was God's spokesman (1 S. 12:16-18). 11. Anointed David as king over Israel (1 S. 16:1, 13). **Predictions and Messages** 1. The prophecy that judgment would fall on the family of Eli, the priest, because of his evil sons (1 S. 3:11-14; 4:17-22). 2. The prophecy that if Israel would get rid of their false gods, the LORD would help Israel defeat the Philistines (1 S.7:3). 3. The prophecy that when Israel cried out to the LORD because of the severe rule of the king they had insisted on, the LORD would not hear them (1 S.8:10-18). (cont. on next page)	**Time** *1095-1015 B.C., about forty years before King Saul and during most of his reign.* **Place** *In the center regions of Israel, serving as judge to the entire nation. In order to hear all the cases and judge Israel rightly, Samuel traveled on a regular yearly circuit all his life from Bethel to Gilgal to Mizpeh and back to his home in Ramah (1 S.7:15-17).*	The messages, ministry and life of Samuel the prophet can be summed up in three words: "Serve the LORD." With this simple message, Samuel guided and judged the people of Israel for eighty years. Samuel encouraged the people: 1. To serve the LORD with all their heart (1 S.12:20, 24). 2. To serve the LORD and not to turn aside (1 S.12:20). 3. To serve the LORD in truth (1 S.12:24). 4. To serve the LORD, considering what great things He had done for them (1 S.12:24). Samuel's testimony is one of the strongest records of faithfulness ever lived. In Samuel's lifetime, he witnessed some of the most horrifying evil and wickedness ever committed upon the face of the earth, even by the leadership of Israel. For example, Eli, the priest who reared and trained him, would not control his own wicked sons. They committed the most vile acts of immorality imaginable—at the very tabernacle itself, the worship center of Israel (1 S.2:22). Saul, whom God had raised up to serve as king, turned out to be a great disappointment. Despite Samuel's great trust in him, Saul disobeyed God time and time again, until God finally had to remove him from the kingship and instruct Samuel to anoint another (David). But Samuel was faithful, faithful to the end. Through all the years he stayed true to the LORD despite all the horrifying evil of society.	Just imagine the impact Samuel's life and ministry had. There was no one, not a single person who could accuse Samuel of wrongdoing. He had lived a righteous life and served faithfully throughout all the years, throughout all the days of his life. What a testimony! What a dynamic, living example for us. We must live righteous lives, keeping all the commandments of God, obeying Him in all that He says. We must be faithful and diligent in all that we do. This is the strong declaration of God's Holy Word: **Now it is required that those who have been given a trust must prove faithful (1 Co.4:2).** **Therefore, my dear brothers, stand firm. Let nothing move you. Always give yourselves fully to the work of the Lord, because you know that your labor in the Lord is not in vain (1 Co.15:58).** **Each one should use whatever gift he has received to serve others, faithfully administering God's grace in its various forms (1 Pe.4:10).** **They will make war against the Lamb, but the Lamb will overcome them because he is Lord of lords and King of kings—and with him will be his called, chosen and faithful followers" (Re.17:14).** **But your hearts must be fully committed to the LORD our God, to live by his decrees and obey his commands, as at this time" (1 K.8:61).**

PROPHET	TIME/PLACE GIVEN	MAIN MESSAGE	PRACTICAL APPLICATION
SAMUEL (cont.) 4. The declaration that Saul's donkeys had been found (1 S.9:20). 5. The prophecy that God would change Saul into a different man so that he could serve as king (1 S.10:6). 6. The sermon of the history of Israel—a strong message that God would be with Israel so long as they faithfully obeyed Him (1 S.12:6-15). 7. The prophecy that the LORD would take Israel out of the promised land if they did evil (1 S. 12:24-25). 8. The declaration that God had rejected Saul and chosen another (David) to be king (1 S.13:13-14; 15:17-29; 28:16-17). 9. The message from God to Samuel, that God was sorry he had made Saul king, because Saul had been so disobedient (1 S.15:10-11). 10. The prophecy that Saul and Jonathan would die the next day in battle (1 S. 28:18-19). **Scripture References** 1 S.1:1-25:1; 28:8-20; Je.15:1		If you fear the LORD and serve and obey him and do not rebel against his commands, and if both you and the king who reigns over you follow the LORD your God—good! But if you do not obey the LORD, and if you rebel against his commands, his hand will be against you, as it was against your fathers...."Do not be afraid," Samuel replied. "You have done all this evil; yet do not turn away from the LORD, but serve the LORD with all your heart. Do not turn away after useless idols. They can do you no good, nor can they rescue you, because they are useless. For the sake of his great name the LORD will not reject his people, because the LORD was pleased to make you his own. As for me, far be it from me that I should sin against the LORD by failing to pray for you. And I will teach you the way that is good and right. But be sure to fear the LORD and serve him faithfully with all your heart; consider what great things he has done for you. Yet if you persist in doing evil, both you and your king will be swept away" (1 S.12:14-15, 20-25). But Samuel replied: "Does the LORD delight in burnt offerings and sacrifices as much as in obeying the voice of the LORD? To obey is better than sacrifice, and to heed is better than the fat of rams. For rebellion is like the sin of divination, and arrogance like the evil of idolatry. Because you have rejected the word of the LORD, he has rejected you as king" (1 S.15:22-23).	

PROPHET	TIME/PLACE GIVEN	MAIN MESSAGE	PRACTICAL APPLICATION
SHEMAIAH **(Jehovah/Yahweh hears)** **Known Facts** 1. Recorded the history of Rehoboam (2 Chr. 11:15). 2. Ministered to Judah, the Southern Kingdom (1 K.12:22; 2 Chr.12:5). **Predictions and Messages** 1. The message to King Rehoboam that the rebellion of Jeroboam and the northern tribes of Israel was the will of God and that Rehoboam should not try to stop the uprising (1 K.12:22-24; 2 Chr.11:2-4). 2. The prophecy that Jerusalem would be given into the hand of Egypt's King Shishak because the people had been unfaithful, forsaking the Law of the LORD (2 Chr.12:5). 3. The prophecy that the people would become servants of Shishak, but Jerusalem would not be destroyed, because the people had repented at the LORD's first message (see #2; 2 Chr.12:7-8). **Scripture References** 1 K.12:22-24; 2 Chr.11:2-4; 12:5-8, 15 (cont. on next page)	**Time** *926 B.C., the fifth year of the reign of Rehoboam, king of Judah.* **Place** *Jerusalem, the capital of Judah, the Southern Kingdom of Israel.*	Shortly after the ten northern tribes had revolted and formed the Northern Kingdom, Rehoboam mobilized an army of 180,000 soldiers to put down the rebellion. His purpose was to invade the northern tribes and permanently subject them under his rule. But while marching north to attack, God's prophet Shemaiah confronted Rehoboam. God's prophet had a stark warning for the king and the leaders of Judah (vv.2-4). They were not to fight against their brothers, the Israelites. Rather they were to return home, for the ruptured, divided kingdom was of God, the work of His hands. Hearing this stern warning from the prophet, the king and the people obeyed the LORD and returned home. But five years later when the scene refocuses upon Rehoboam and Judah, tragic differences are seen in the life of the king and people. They have turned away from the LORD, disobeying His Word and committing apostasy against Him. The hearts of Rehoboam and the people have wandered away from the LORD. As a result Shemaiah, the prophet, had another message for the king and people: Shishak, the Egyptian king was going to destroy Jerusalem. Upon hearing this message, the leaders quickly humbled themselves before the LORD. Thus God sent Shemaiah back with an amended message: Shishak would still attack and some of the people would be taken away as slaves, but the city of Jerusalem would remain. Note: the more severe judgment of God was averted because the people repented, but they still suffered the consequences for their sin. **But this word of God came to Shemaiah the man of God: "Say to Rehoboam son of Solomon king of Judah, to the whole house of Judah and Benjamin, and to the rest of the people, 'This is what the LORD says: Do not go up to fight against your brothers, the Israelites. Go home, every one of you, for this is my doing.'" So they obeyed the word of the LORD and went home again, as the LORD had ordered (1 K.12:22-24).**	God demands obedience, a lifetime of obedience. We are to always obey God's Holy Word, His commandments. Obeying God today and disobeying Him tomorrow does not make us acceptable to God. A life of inconsistency—obeying this week and disobeying next week—exposes a heart of insincerity and hypocrisy, a heart of dishonesty before God. A true profession of Christ means that we keep God's Word, obey His holy commandments. When we keep some commandments now and break other commandments later and continue a path of inconsistency, this is a life of deception and duplicity. Professing to be a follower of the LORD and consistently breaking His commandments is living a double life. It is attempting to establish a relationship with the LORD that is phony, double-dealing, shifty—a fake life that professes to obey God by living an unfaithful, untruthful life—a hypocritical life. **"Not everyone who says to me, 'Lord, Lord,' will enter the kingdom of heaven, but only he who does the will of my Father who is in heaven. Many will say to me on that day, 'Lord, Lord, did we not prophesy in your name, and in your name drive out demons and perform many miracles?' Then I will tell them plainly, 'I never knew you. Away from me, you evildoers!' (Mt.7:21-23).** **You are my friends if you do what I command (Jn.15:14).** **Oh, that their hearts would be inclined to fear me and keep all my commands always, so that it might go well with them and their children forever! (De.5:29).** **Come near to God and he will come near to you. Wash your hands, you sinners, and purify your hearts, you double-minded (Js.4:8).**

PROPHET	TIME/PLACE GIVEN	MAIN MESSAGE	PRACTICAL APPLICATION
SHEMAIAH (cont.)		Then the prophet Shemaiah came to Rehoboam and to the leaders of Judah who had assembled in Jerusalem for fear of Shishak, and he said to them, "This is what the LORD says, 'You have abandoned me; therefore, I now abandon you to Shishak.'" The leaders of Israel and the king humbled themselves and said, "The LORD is just." When the LORD saw that they humbled themselves, this word of the LORD came to Shemaiah: "Since they have humbled themselves, I will not destroy them but will soon give them deliverance. My wrath will not be poured out on Jerusalem through Shishak. They will, however, become subject to him, so that they may learn the difference between serving me and serving the kings of other lands" (2 Chr.12:5-8).	

PROPHET	TIME/PLACE GIVEN	MAIN MESSAGE	PRACTICAL APPLICATION
The **UNNAMED PROPHET** **who prophesied total victory for King Ahab of Israel over the Arameans (Syrians)** **Known Facts** Delivered a message from God to King Ahab (1 K. 20:28). **Predictions and Messages** The entire Aramean (Syrian) army would be given into the hand of King Ahab. **Scripture References** 1 K.20:26-30	**Time** *855 B.C., during the reign of Ahab of Israel and during the ministry of Elijah the prophet.* **Place** *Samaria, the capital of the Northern Kingdom of Israel.*	The LORD sent His prophet to King Ahab once more to announce that He would deliver the vast army of the Arameans (Syrians) into the hands of the Israelites. Through the victory Ahab was to learn a great truth: The LORD is sovereign; His power is not partial or limited, but absolute. The LORD was going to prove that He was not just one god among many, not just a god of the hills as the Syrians falsely believed. He alone is the LORD (Jehovah/Yahweh), the only true and living God. **The man of God came up and told the king of Israel, "This is what the LORD says: 'Because the Arameans think the LORD is a god of the hills and not a god of the valleys, I will deliver this vast army into your hands, and you will know that I am the LORD.'" (1 K.20:28).**	The lesson for us is a much needed one: The LORD's sovereignty (His power) is not limited or partial, but absolute. The LORD is sovereign everywhere, throughout the entire universe. He is sovereign over all nations and kingdoms upon earth and in heaven. No limitation whatsoever hampers God's sovereignty or power. God controls all events and all happenings. And His sovereign power will eventually end all evil. **For he must reign until he has put all his enemies under his feet (1 Co.15:25).** **The LORD will reign for ever and ever" (Ex.15:18).** **The LORD has established his throne in heaven, and his kingdom rules over all (Ps. 103:19).**

THE PROPHETS

PROPHET	TIME/PLACE GIVEN	MAIN MESSAGE	PRACTICAL APPLICATION
The **UNNAMED PROPHET** who prophesied a victory for King Ahab of Israel over the Arameans (Syrians) **Known Facts** Delivered two messages from God to King Ahab (1 K.20:13, 22). **Predictions and Messages** 1. The prophecy that the LORD would deliver the Arameans (Syrians) into the hand of King Ahab (1 K. 20:13-15). 2. The prophecy that the Arameans would attack again the next year (1 K.20:22). **Scripture References** 1 K.20:1-25	**Time** *856 B.C., during the reign of Ahab of Israel and during the ministry of Elijah the prophet.* **Place** *Samaria, the capital of the Northern Kingdom of Israel.*	The LORD sent His prophet to King Ahab with a very special message during a very difficult time. The massive Syrian army was surrounding Ahab's capital city of Samaria. The situation seemed utterly hopeless. But the LORD longed to reach the heart of Ahab, longed for Ahab to stop Jezebel's savage purge of God's prophets and the worship of the LORD. Thus the LORD sent an unnamed prophet to Ahab, announcing that God was going to give a miraculous victory to the king for one specific purpose: to prove that He alone is God, the only true and living God. Ahab followed the battle instructions given him and achieved a great victory. Later, after the battle, the prophet came again and warned Ahab that the Arameans would attack again the next year. Now note this fact: even this warning should have aroused Ahab to repent, for God was still reaching out to him in compassion, patiently longing for him to turn from his wickedness, to acknowledge the one and only true God. But Ahab's heart was stubborn and unyielding. **Meanwhile a prophet came to Ahab king of Israel and announced, "This is what the LORD says: 'Do you see this vast army? I will give it into your hand today, and then you will know that I am the LORD.'" "But who will do this?" asked Ahab. The prophet replied, "This is what the LORD says: 'The young officers of the provincial commanders will do it.'" "And who will start the battle?" he asked. The prophet answered, "You will." So Ahab summoned the young officers of the provincial commanders, 232 men. Then he assembled the rest of the Israelites, 7,000 in all (1 K.20:13-15).** **Afterward, the prophet came to the king of Israel and said, "Strengthen your position and see what must be done, because next spring the king of Aram will attack you again" (1 K.20:22).**	God's purpose for helping us in times of trouble is to prove that He alone is God. There is only one true and living God, only one Creator, only one Sovereign LORD and Majesty of the universe. All other gods are false, deceivers that mislead and entrap human beings and capture their loyalty. And the terrible tragedy is this: if we are deceived into following and worshipping false gods, we condemn and doom ourselves. When hardships and misfortunes fall upon us, there is no living God to help us; for we are following false gods that are lifeless and powerless to help. We must recognize the LORD, the only true God. We must trust in the only One Who can help us in time of trouble. **You alone are the LORD. You made the heavens, even the highest heavens, and all their starry host, the earth and all that is on it, the seas and all that is in them. You give life to everything, and the multitudes of heaven worship you (Neh.9:6).** **In the beginning you laid the foundations of the earth, and the heavens are the work of your hands (Ps.102:25).** **"I issue a decree that in every part of my kingdom people must fear and reverence the God of Daniel. "For he is the living God and he endures forever; his kingdom will not be destroyed, his dominion will never end (Da.6:26).** **The salvation of the righteous comes from the LORD; he is their stronghold in time of trouble (Ps.37:39).**

THE PROPHETS

PROPHET	TIME/PLACE GIVEN	MAIN MESSAGE	PRACTICAL APPLICATION
The UNNAMED PROPHET who rebuked Eli and his house for profaning the temple of the LORD **Known Facts** Delivered a message to Eli the priest (1 S.2:27-34). **Predictions and Messages** 1. The prophecy that each generation of Eli's family would be stricken so that all the men would die in the prime of life (1 S. 2:27-33; esp. v.31). 2. The prophecy that Eli's sons would both die in the same day—a sign that the prophecy concerning Eli's family would come true (1 S.2:34). 3. The prophecy that the LORD would raise up a faithful priest in place of Eli (1 S.2:35-36). **Scripture References** 1 S.2:12-36	**Time** *1085 B.C., when Eli, the priest, was an old man.* **Place** *Shiloh, the central place of worship in Israel prior to the rule of the kings.*	An unnamed prophet was sent by God to pronounce the terrifying judgment against the priestly family of Eli. All three of his sons who were priests, would soon die, and the priesthood of Eli's family was to be transferred to the family of a faithful priest. The unnamed prophet declared three things: 1. He challenged Eli and his sons to remember the history of the priesthood. He pointed out what a privilege it was for priests to approach God and present the offerings to him. For the offerings symbolized the redemption of God's people through the blood of the sacrifice. 2. He pronounced the charge of God against Eli and his sons—that they had scorned the holy things of God and committed immorality. 3. He pronounced the judgment of God against Eli and his sons. The wickedness of Eli and his sons had been so horrible that God was left with no choice. He had to cut them off as priests. **Now a man of God came to Eli and said to him, "This is what the LORD says: 'Did I not clearly reveal myself to your father's house when they were in Egypt under Pharaoh?...Why do you scorn my sacrifice and offering that I prescribed for my dwelling? Why do you honor your sons more than me by fattening yourselves on the choice parts of every offering made by my people Israel?' "Therefore the LORD, the God of Israel, declares: 'I promised that your house and your father's house would minister before me forever.' But now the LORD declares: 'Far be it from me! Those who honor me I will honor, but those who despise me will be disdained. The time is coming when I will cut short your strength and the strength of your father's house, so that there will not be an old man in your family line.... "'And what happens to your two sons, Hophni and Phinehas, will be a sign to you—they will both die on the same day. I will raise up for myself a faithful priest, who will do according to what is** (cont. in column 4)	Judgment upon the immoral and wicked of this world will definitely take place. This is the strong prophetic message of God's Word. Just when the judgment of God is going to fall upon this world is unknown. Just when each of us is going to stand before God, even the minister, is unknown. But the day is definitely coming. The only sure thing that we know about our lives is this: we will die and after that will be the judgment. Judgment is sure, definite, and absolutely certain. Judgment is coming. **Just as man is destined to die once, and after that to face judgment (He.9:27).** **"When the Son of Man comes in his glory, and all the angels with him, he will sit on his throne in heavenly glory. All the nations will be gathered before him, and he will separate the people one from another as a shepherd separates the sheep from the goats. He will put the sheep on his right and the goats on his left (Mt.25:31-33).** (cont. from col.3) **in my heart and mind. I will firmly establish his house, and he will minister before my anointed one always. Then everyone left in your family line will come and bow down before him for a piece of silver and a crust of bread and plead, "Appoint me to some priestly office so I can have food to eat."'" (1 S.2:27, 29-31, 34-36)**

THE PROPHETS

PROPHET	TIME/PLACE GIVEN	MAIN MESSAGE	PRACTICAL APPLICATION
The **UNNAMED PROPHET** who rebuked Israel for fearing the false gods of the Amorites **Known Facts** Delivered a message to the Israelites (Jud.6:8-10). **Predictions and Messages** The message that Israel had been disobedient because they were in fear of the Amorites (Jud.6:8-10). **Scripture References** Jud.6:7-10	**Time** *Approximately 1210 B.C., during the oppression of the Israelites by the Amorites.* **Place** *The southern regions of Israel.*	The LORD raised up a prophet to rebuke the Israelites because the Israelites needed to be warned as never before. For generations, the Israelites had been failing God, turning back time and again to the sins and evil of their neighbors and engaging in their false worship. The prophet rebuked Israel for four specific sins or evils: ➢ The Israelites had forgotten God's salvation, His wonderful deliverance from Egyptian slavery. ➢ The Israelites had forgotten God's deliverance down through the centuries from their oppressors and forgotten His gift of the promised land. ➢ The Israelites had forsaken God, engaging in false worship or idolatry. ➢ The Israelites had refused to listen to God, disobeying Him and breaking His commandments. **He sent them a prophet, who said, "This is what the LORD, the God of Israel, says: I brought you up out of Egypt, out of the land of slavery. I snatched you from the power of Egypt and from the hand of all your oppressors. I drove them from before you and gave you their land. I said to you, 'I am the LORD your God; do not worship the gods of the Amorites, in whose land you live.' But you have not listened to me" (Jud.6:8-10).**	If we continue in sin—walk day by day disobeying God—a strong rebuke and correction are needed. We need to be awakened, stirred, aroused out of our slumber and hardness of sin. When we sincerely confess our sins and repent, God will deliver us. But we need to learn one truth: we are not to return to our sin. The sin is to be forsaken or left behind, and we are to walk forward, growing more and more in the righteousness of God. If we return to the same sin time and again, continuing in sin, we deserve to be rebuked. **Jesus replied, "No one who puts his hand to the plow and looks back is fit for service in the kingdom of God." (Lu.9:62).** **Have nothing to do with the fruitless deeds of darkness, but rather expose them (Ep. 5:11).** **Those who sin are to be rebuked publicly, so that the others may take warning (1 Ti.5:20).**

PROPHET	TIME/PLACE GIVEN	MAIN MESSAGE	PRACTICAL APPLICATION
The UNNAMED PROPHET who rebuked King Ahab of Israel for sparing Ben-Hadad, the evil king of Aram (Syria) **Known Facts** 1. Belonged to the school of the prophets (1 K.20:35). 2. Delivered a message to King Ahab (1 K. 20:39-42). 3. Was known as a prophet (1 K.20:41). **Predictions and Messages** 1. The prophecy that a fellow prophet would be killed by a lion (1 K.20:36). 2. The message that King Ahab had done evil by sparing Ben-Hadad, the evil king of Aram (1 K.20:39-42). **Scripture References** 1 K.20:31-43	**Time** *855 B.C., during the reign of Ahab of Israel and during the ministry of Elijah the prophet.* **Place** *Samaria, the capital of the Northern Kingdom of Israel.*	Under God's instructions, an unnamed prophet sought to disguise himself in order to confront King Ahab. The unnamed prophet ordered a fellow prophet to strike him so that he would appear to be a wounded soldier when he confronted the king. But the fellow prophet refused. As a result, the unnamed prophet predicted the other prophet's death. The next man obeyed and struck the unnamed prophet, wounding him so that his disguise would not be questioned. Disguised as a wounded soldier, the unnamed prophet waited by the road for the king. When Ahab finally arrived and was passing by, the unnamed prophet cried out for a pardon. He told the king that he was in trouble because he had let a prisoner escape. Ahab demonstrated his hard heart by condemning the man. As soon as Ahab had issued his verdict, the prophet stripped off his disguise and pronounced God's condemnation upon Ahab for letting Ben-Hadad, the evil king of Syria, go free. Ahab's life would be demanded in place of the life of Ben-Hadad. **So the prophet said, "Because you have not obeyed the LORD, as soon as you leave me a lion will kill you." And after the man went away, a lion found him and killed him (1 K.20:36).** **As the king passed by, the prophet called out to him, "Your servant went into the thick of the battle, and someone came to me with a captive and said, 'Guard this man. If he is missing, it will be your life for his life, or you must pay a talent of silver.' While your servant was busy here and there, the man disappeared." "That is your sentence," the king of Israel said. "You have pronounced it yourself" (1 K.20:39-40).**	The lesson we need to learn is that disobedience has consequences. If we disobey God, we stand condemned and will bear the hand of God's judgment. In giving the commandments, God intended good for us. The commandments tell us how to live good, honorable and productive lives that are victorious and conquering. Through obedience, we can live lives that prove to be successful and that bring a sense of fulfillment and satisfaction to the human heart. **And give relief to you who are troubled, and to us as well. This will happen when the Lord Jesus is revealed from heaven in blazing fire with his powerful angels. He will punish those who do not know God and do not obey the gospel of our Lord Jesus. They will be punished with everlasting destruction and shut out from the presence of the Lord and from the majesty of his power (2 Th.1:7-9).** **But if you do not obey the LORD, and if you rebel against his commands, his hand will be against you, as it was against your fathers (1 S.12:15).** **The curse if you disobey the commands of the LORD your God and turn from the way that I command you today by following other gods, which you have not known (De.11:28).**

THE PROPHETS

PROPHET	TIME/PLACE GIVEN	MAIN MESSAGE	PRACTICAL APPLICATION
The UNNAMED PROPHET who rebuked **King Amaziah of Judah for his idolatry** **Known Facts** Delivered a message to King Amaziah of Judah. **Predictions and Messages** 1. The rebuke of King Amaziah for foolishly worshipping the gods of the Edomites (2 Chr.25:15). 2. The prophecy that King Amaziah would be destroyed because he would not listen to the message of the prophet (2 Chr.25:16). **Scripture References** 2 Chr.25:14-16	**Time** *767 B.C., the last year of the reign of King Amaziah of Judah.* **Place** *Jerusalem, the capital of the Southern Kingdom of Judah.*	Almost unbelievably and certainly tragically, Amaziah committed the terrible sin of false worship. As part of the plunder from his victory, the king brought back the idols of Edom, set them up and worshipped them. Why would King Amaziah commit such folly, turning away from the LORD to false idols? Perhaps King Amaziah began to think that he actually had the support of these false gods so he began to worship them in thanksgiving for the victory he had achieved. The anger of the LORD was aroused and burned against Amaziah. God sent a prophet to warn the king by asking him a question: why had the king worshipped false gods, gods that could not save their own people from the hand of Amaziah? Reacting in rage, the king rejected the prophetic warning and threatened the prophet if he continued issuing his message of rebuke. But fearlessly, the prophet issued a final warning: God would judge and destroy the king for his sin and for not heeding the warning. **The anger of the LORD burned against Amaziah, and he sent a prophet to him, who said, "Why do you consult this people's gods, which could not save their own people from your hand?" While he was still speaking, the king said to him, "Have we appointed you an adviser to the king? Stop! Why be struck down?" So the prophet stopped but said, "I know that God has determined to destroy you, because you have done this and have not listened to my counsel" (2 Chr.25:15-16).**	Believers must guard and keep themselves from idols. What does this mean? An idol is anything that takes first place in a person's life, anything that a person puts before God. An idol is anything that consumes man's focus and concentration, anything that consumes his energy and efforts more than God. A person can make an idol out of anything in this world; a person can take anything and worship it before God; he can allow it to consume his mind and thoughts and life: ➤ houses ➤ cars ➤ lands ➤ boats ➤ job ➤ sports ➤ position ➤ money ➤ spouse ➤ comfort ➤ children ➤ television ➤ sex ➤ possessions ➤ food ➤ pleasures ➤ power ➤ recreation But idols are not gods, no matter what their worshipers may think. There is no other God but One. It is true that people call out to gods, but... • they are gods of their own minds and imaginations, ideas and notions. • they are gods of wood and stone. • they are gods and lords of their own creation. • they have no power to save or deliver. **Dear children, keep yourselves from idols (1 Jn.5:21).** **Although they claimed to be wise, they became fools and exchanged the glory of the immortal God for images made to look like mortal man and birds and animals and reptiles (Ro.1:22-23).**

THE PROPHETS

PROPHET	TIME/PLACE GIVEN	MAIN MESSAGE	PRACTICAL APPLICATION
The **UNNAMED PROPHET** who rebuked King Jeroboam I for his idolatry **Known Facts** 1. Lived in Judah (1 K. 13:1). 2. Prayed for King Jeroboam and the king's withered hand was healed (1 K.13:6). 3. Commanded by God not to delay—not even to eat or drink—while on his mission (1 K. 13:9). 4. Broke the command of God by visiting and having a meal with an old prophet (1 K.13:19). 5. Was killed by a lion because he disobeyed God's command (1 K.13:24). **Predictions and Messages** 1. The prophecy that a king named Josiah would execute all the false prophets on the altar at Bethel which King Jeroboam had set up for idolatry (1 K.13:2). 2. The prophecy that the altar at Bethel would split apart (1 K.13:3). **Scripture References** 1 K.13:1-25; 2 K.23:15-20	**Time** *931 B.C., the first year of the reign of King Jeroboam I, when the country of Israel had just split into two nations, the Northern Kingdom of Israel and the Southern Kingdom of Judah.* **Place** *Bethel, just north of Jerusalem.*	Just as King Jeroboam was standing by the altar he had set up at Bethel, getting ready to present a false sacrifice, he was suddenly confronted by a young unnamed prophet. The young man prophesied against the altar of false worship established by Jeroboam. The altar and its priests would be destroyed by a future descendant of David named Josiah. To prove that this event would take place, the young prophet gave Jeroboam a sign. The altar would immediately be split apart by the power of God Himself and the ashes would pour out. And so it happened. Pointing to the young man, Jeroboam ordered his guards to arrest him. Instead, another shocking sign happened, which abruptly interrupted the arrest. Jeroboam's hand immediately withered. Terrified, Jeroboam pleaded with the prophet for help. The prophet prayed for the king and his hand was restored. **He cried out against the altar by the word of the LORD: "O altar, altar! This is what the LORD says: 'A son named Josiah will be born to the house of David. On you he will sacrifice the priests of the high places who now make offerings here, and human bones will be burned on you.'" That same day the man of God gave a sign: "This is the sign the LORD has declared: The altar will be split apart and the ashes on it will be poured out." (1 K.13:2-3).**	The lesson for us is strikingly clear: idolatry and false worship do not please the LORD. God totally opposes idolatry and false worship. Idols are not just images made out of wood, stone, metal or some other material. We can make an idol out of anything, for idols are anything that captures our heart more than God. Whatever captivates our hearts, whatever the focus of our hearts is, whatever we give our hearts to, that person or thing becomes our god, our idol. For that person or thing possesses our hearts, our primary interest and attention. As a result, God is denied, ignored or forgotten. **The wrath of God is being revealed from heaven against all the godlessness and wickedness of men who suppress the truth by their wickedness....They exchanged the truth of God for a lie, and worshiped and served created things rather than the Creator—who is forever praised. Amen (Ro. 1:18, 25).** **"You shall not make for yourself an idol in the form of anything in heaven above or on the earth beneath or in the waters below (Ex.20:4).** **Be careful, or you will be enticed to turn away and worship other gods and bow down to them (De.11:16).**

PROPHET	TIME/PLACE GIVEN	MAIN MESSAGE	PRACTICAL APPLICATION
The UNNAMED PROPHET who warned **King Amaziah of Judah not to hire the army of Israel** **Known Facts** Delivered a message to King Amaziah. **Predictions and Messages** 1. The warning that King Amaziah of Judah will meet with disaster if he deploys the troops of Israel into battle (2 Chr. 25:7-8). 2. The message that God has the power to help or to bring defeat (2 Chr.25:8). 3. The message that God is able to supply far more than anything ever lost (2 Chr.25:9). **Scripture References** 2 Chr.25:5-10	**Time** *767 B.C., the last year of the reign of King Amaziah of Judah.* **Place** *Jerusalem, the capital of the Southern Kingdom of Judah.*	King Amaziah of Judah was preparing for war against the age-old enemy of Israel, the Edomites. Amaziah had just hired the armies of Israel to assist him in his battles. But before he could deploy these troops, Amaziah was confronted by a prophet of the LORD who issued a strong warning to the king. The prophet told King Amaziah that he must not allow Israel's mercenary troops to march with him. For the LORD was not with Israel. Living wicked lives and engaging in false worship, the people of the Northern Kingdom had rejected the LORD and were no longer placing their hope in the eternal covenant given to David. They had abandoned the LORD; consequently, the LORD had abandoned them. Still speaking to Amaziah, the prophet continued his warning. If the king marched into battle with the Israelite mercenary soldiers, he would be defeated. Even if he fought courageously against the Edomites, the LORD would make sure he was defeated. For the LORD has the power to help or to overthrow an army. The prophet further assured King Amaziah that God would provide far more plunder—more than enough—to cover his losses if he would just discharge the unbelieving troops. **But a man of God came to him and said, "O king, these troops from Israel must not march with you, for the LORD is not with Israel—not with any of the people of Ephraim. Even if you go and fight courageously in battle, God will overthrow you before the enemy, for God has the power to help or to overthrow." Amaziah asked the man of God, "But what about the hundred talents I paid for these Israelite troops?" The man of God replied, "The LORD can give you much more than that" (2 Chr.25:7-9).**	Believers are to turn away from evil associations. Close associations always influence us. If we fellowship with godly people, we will be influenced by godliness. But if we fellowship with ungodly people, their ungodliness will influence us. It is impossible to escape the influence of close associations. We all influence each other; and the more closely we are associated, the more we are influenced. If a believer associates with the wicked, eventually the wicked will encourage the believer to join him in his sinful behavior. A godly person is always pulled down, influenced negatively by close associations with those who smoke, take drugs, get drunk, or engage in immoral behav-ior. No matter who we are or how strong we may be, we will be strongly influenced to participate in the sinful behavior. For this reason the LORD commands us to live lives of *spiritual separation*. Believers are not to fellowship nor become closely associated with the wicked and evil of this earth. We are to be spiritually separated. Living upon the earth, we are to be friends with everyone, unbeliever as well as believer. And we are to be kind, caring, and helpful to everyone. But we are not to form close alliances, associations, or bonds with the wicked and evil of this earth. **But now I am writing you that you must not associate with anyone who calls himself a brother but is sexually immoral or greedy, an idolater or a slanderer, a drunkard or a swindler. With such a man do not even eat (1 Co.5:11).** **"Do not follow the crowd in doing wrong. When you give testimony in a lawsuit, do not pervert justice by siding with the crowd (Ex.23:2).**

PROPHET	TIME/PLACE GIVEN	MAIN MESSAGE	PRACTICAL APPLICATION
URIJAH (Jehovah/Yahweh is a Light) **Known Facts** 1. Was the son of Shemaiah (Je.26:20). 2. Lived in Kiriath-Jearim (Je.26:20). 3. Prophesied in Judah (Je.26:20-21). 4. Fled to Egypt to escape execution by King Jehoiakim (Je.26:21). 5. Was brought back from Egypt by the king's men and slain (Je.26:22-23). 6. Given the burial of a common criminal (Je.26:23). **Predictions and Messages** Preached messages similar to those of Jeremiah the prophet (Je.26:20). **Scripture References** Je.26:20-23	**Time** *608 B.C., at the beginning of the reign of Jehoiakim, king of Judah.* **Place** *Jerusalem, the capital city of Judah, in the palace of the king.*	All that is known about the messages of Urijah is that they were similar to those of Jeremiah, the prophet. By this one fact, we can know something of what Urijah prophesied. First, Urijah was bound to be a true prophet, proclaiming the messages given him by God. He was not speaking the popular, conscience-soothing messages of the false prophets of that time. Second, Urijah was courageous, warning both king and citizen to repent of their wickedness and false worship or else face the judgment of God. Otherwise, why would the king be so angry and determined to have Urijah executed? Third, we can be sure that Urijah preached the truth of God's Word right up until the day of his martyrdom. **(Now Uriah son of Shemaiah from Kiriath Jearim was another man who prophesied in the name of the LORD; he prophesied the same things against this city and this land as Jeremiah did (Je.26:20).**	The preacher must not compromise the Word of God. He must say exactly what God gives him to say. After all, the message is not his, but God's. It is not his to change or alter in the least. Even if it means death, the man of God must not give another message or a watered down version of the truth. He must not seek to say what is popular or more acceptable to his listeners. He must preach the whole counsel of God without regard to circumstances or popular opinion. He must say exactly what God gives him to say. **He said to them, "Go into all the world and preach the good news to all creation (Mk. 16:15).** **Day after day, in the temple courts and from house to house, they never stopped teaching and proclaiming the good news that Jesus is the Christ (Ac.5:42).** **But we preach Christ crucified: a stumbling block to Jews and foolishness to Gentiles (1 Co.1:23).** **Yet when I preach the gospel, I cannot boast, for I am compelled to preach. Woe to me if I do not preach the gospel! (1 Co.9:16).** **Preach the Word; be prepared in season and out of season; correct, rebuke and encourage—with great patience and careful instruction (2 Ti.4:2).**

PROPHET	TIME/PLACE GIVEN	MAIN MESSAGE	PRACTICAL APPLICATION
ZECHARIAH (Jehovah/Yahweh has brought to mind), the son of Jehoiada **Known Facts** 1. Was the son of Jehoiada, the priest (2 Chr.24:20). 2. Was stoned to death because of his message (2 Chr.24:21). **Predictions and Messages** The message that the LORD had forsaken the people of Judah because they had forsaken the LORD and his commandments by their false worship and idolatry (2 Chr. 24:20). **Scripture References** 2 Chr.24:17-22; Mt. 23:34-39; Lu.11:47-51	**Time** *797 B.C., a year before the death of Joash, king of Judah.* **Place** *Jerusalem, the capital city of Judah.*	After the death of Jehoiada, the priest, King Joash, who had led a tremendous revival and spiritual reformation in his younger years, slipped away from the LORD and committed terrible apostasy. Joash listened and gave in to wicked, influential leaders who were false worshipers. Because of their terrible apostasy of turning away to false worship, they stood guilty before the LORD and aroused His anger. God sent prophet after prophet to warn the king, but the king and people stubbornly rejected the prophets of God, refusing to listen to their warnings and refusing to repent. In mercy, however, the LORD made one last attempt to get Joash and the people to repent. The Spirit of the LORD came upon Zechariah with a very special message for the king and the people. They had disobeyed God's commandments and forsaken Him; consequently, the LORD had now forsaken them. But in the depth of their stubborn, stiff-necked rebellion, they still did not repent. Instead, they actually murdered the prophet Zechariah. Furious over the pronouncement of judgment against them, Joash ordered the prophet stoned to death in the very courtyard of the temple itself. Looking up into the eyes of the king as he lay dying, Zechariah pronounced a divine curse upon the king and the people. They were to soon face God's vengeance. The next year, the Arameans (Syrians) attacked and overran the countryside. Joash was killed in battle. **Then the Spirit of God came upon Zechariah son of Jehoiada the priest. He stood before the people and said, "This is what God says: 'Why do you disobey the LORD's commands? You will not prosper. Because you have forsaken the LORD, he has forsaken you'" (2 Chr.24:20).**	How many people have a wonderful beginning in life but a terrible ending? Think of people who have walked through many years of life with upright characters, living honest, moral, and just lives. Yet in the latter years of their lives their character has declined, deteriorated. Some have become immoral and dishonest, even cheating other people. Others are no longer kind and gracious but, rather, unkind, mean-spirited, and reactionary, sometimes even cursing or assaulting those who love and care for them. Whereas they used to live righteous lives and profess to be followers of the LORD, they are now backsliding, living carnal, fleshly lives. They not only ignore the LORD but they also deny Him. They curse His name, use profanity, and tell off-colored jokes. They no longer worship the LORD or are faithful in church attendance. Instead of setting the example that we must listen to the Word of God being taught, they slip into immorality, tearing out the hearts of parents, wives, husbands, children, former pastors, and teachers. Far too many who begin with Christ eventually turn away from Him, committing terrible apostasy against Him. **Because of the increase of wickedness, the love of most will grow cold (Mt.24:12).** **Those on the rock are the ones who receive the word with joy when they hear it, but they have no root. They believe for a while, but in the time of testing they fall away (Lu.8:13).** **But now that you know God—or rather are known by God—how is it that you are turning back to those weak and miserable principles? Do you wish to be enslaved by them all over again? (Ga.4:9).** **Do not harden your hearts as you did in the rebellion, during the time of testing in the desert, where your fathers tested and tried me and for forty years saw what I did. That is why I was angry with that generation, and I said, 'Their hearts are always going astray, and they have not known my ways.' So I declared on oath in my anger, 'They shall never enter my rest.'" See to it, brothers, that none of you has a sinful, unbelieving heart that turns away from the living God (He.3:8-12).**

PROPHET	TIME/PLACE GIVEN	MAIN MESSAGE	PRACTICAL APPLICATION
ZECHARIAH (Jehovah/Yahweh has brought to mind), the son of Berechiah **Known Facts** 1. Was the son of Berechiah, the priest (Zec. 1:1). 2. Was the grandson of Iddo, the priest (Ezr. 6:14). 3. Ministered at the same time as Haggai, the prophet (Ezr.5:1; 6:14). 4. Prophesied in Jerusalem after the return from captivity (Zec. 1:1; Ezr.6:16). 5. Helped to restore the temple (Ezr.6:14-15). 6. Saw startling visions of the end times (Zec. 1:7-6:8). **Predictions and Messages** 1. The sermon that the people needed to repent and turn to the LORD (Zec.1:2-6). 2. The vision of the horseman beside the myrtle trees—the promise of restoration of the temple and to Jerusalem (Zec.1:7-17). 3. The vision of the four horns and the four craftsmen—the prophecy of future world powers (Zec.1:18-21). 4. The vision of a man with a measuring line—the prophecy of divine protection for Jerusalem (Zec.2). 5. The vision of Joshua the High Priest being accused and slandered by Satan—a prophecy of the redemption for all Israel (Zec.3). 6. The prophecy of the Messiah, the Savior of the world, the Righteous Branch Who would take away the sins of the land and bring peace (Is.11:1; Zec.3:8-10; Mt.2:23). (cont. on next page)	**Time** *520–518 B.C., during the reign of Darius the Mede, when the Israelites had returned from captivity.* **Place** *Jerusalem, the capital city of the remnant of Israel.*	The people of Israel had just come out of foreign captivity and badly needed to have a strong sense of direction. Zechariah, along with Haggai, the prophet, immediately pointed them to God, greatly encouraging the people to restore the temple so that it might be worthy to be used to worship the LORD. Now it was not just a building project that Zechariah was leading. As a spiritual leader of thousands of exiles who had just returned from captivity, Zechariah realized the great importance of quickly calling the people to genuine worship. He had to ground them firmly in the LORD right away. And so Zechariah encouraged the people time and again to turn to the LORD with their whole heart, to worship the Great Shepherd of their souls. Zechariah helped to lead a very great revival. His many visions and prophecies emphasized the love of a sovereign God for His people, and His desire to uphold them and work in their behalf. For those who were determined to serve God wholeheartedly, they would be supported and sustained by the LORD. He would bring about marvelous things in their future. **Therefore tell the people: This is what the LORD Almighty says: 'Return to me,' declares the LORD Almighty, 'and I will return to you,' says the LORD Almighty (Zec.1:3).** **This is what the LORD Almighty says: "You who now hear these words spoken by the prophets who were there when the foundation was laid for the house of the LORD Almighty, let your hands be strong so that the temple may be built (Zec.8:9).**	God is sovereign. He rules over the entire universe. But a person should not think that God is far off in outer space someplace. Coming out of terrible tragedy, it is easy for a person to feel that God is a billion miles away. After a tragedy, it is difficult to have a sense of direction. But it is during hardship that a person needs to seek God like never before and to draw close to Him for understanding, for God cares about our problems. We must always be aware that God is not an unconcerned observer of the world He created. He truly cares about every struggle we go through, and He longs to move in our lives to make the future better, much better than our past. God did not just create the world, wind it up and leave it on its own to fly throughout space with man making out the best he can. God is interested and concerned with the world—so much so that He came to earth in human flesh to show how vitally concerned He is. God would not leave man to grope and grasp in the dark. His call to repentance is not for the purpose of pushing man down but to bring him up, to show man that there is a bright future ahead for those who determine to wholeheartedly serve the LORD. **Jesus answered, "I am the way and the truth and the life. No one comes to the Father except through me (Jn.14:6).** **In my distress I called to the LORD; I called out to my God. From his temple he heard my voice; my cry came to his ears (2 S.22:7).** **When you are in distress and all these things have happened to you, then in later days you will return to the LORD your God and obey him. For the LORD your God is a merciful God; he will not abandon or destroy you or forget the covenant with your forefathers, which he confirmed to them by oath (De.4:30-31).**

PROPHET	TIME/PLACE GIVEN	MAIN MESSAGE	PRACTICAL APPLICATION
ZECHARIAH (cont.) 7. The vision of a golden lampstand and two olive trees—the prophecy of continual anointing for Zerubbabel, who was a type of Christ (Zec.4). 8. The vision of a flying scroll—a declaration that wickedness will be purged from the land (Zec.5:1-4). 9. The vision of a woman in a basket—the prophecy of the rebellion of Babylon in the end times (Zec. 5:5-11). 10. The vision of four chariots—the declaration of God's sovereignty over all nations (Zec.6:1-8). 11. A sermon about the proper attitude for religious ceremony (Zec. 7:4-7). 12. A sermon about loving your neighbor (Zec.7:8-14). 13. The prophecy of God's favor coming upon Jerusalem and Judah (Zec.8:1-17). 14. The prophecy of the salvation of the Gentiles (Zec.8:18-23). 15. The prophecy of God's judgment upon Judah's enemies (Zec. 9:1-10). 16. The prophecy of the Christ's kingly declaration—that the Messiah, the Savior of the world, would enter Jerusalem riding on a young donkey (Zec.9:9; Mt.21:1-11). (Cont. in col.3) **Scripture References** The book of *Zechariah*; Ezr.5:1; 6:14; 8:3, 11, 16		**Predictions and Messages** (cont. from col.1) 17. The prophecy of restoration to all Israel (Zec.9:11–10:12). 18. The illustration of two shepherds' staffs—a prophecy of the rejection of the Messiah, the Great Shepherd (Zec.11). 19. The prophecy that the Messiah, the Savior of the world, would be betrayed for thirty pieces of silver (Zec.11:13). 20. The prophecy that Israel will never again abandon the LORD (Zec.12:1–13:9). 21. The prophecy that the Jews will recognize Jesus Christ as the true Messiah, as their true Savior, in the last days (Zec.12:10-14). 22. The prophecy that in the end times, the LORD will be the only king on the earth (Zec.14).	

PROPHET	TIME/PLACE GIVEN	MAIN MESSAGE	PRACTICAL APPLICATION
ZEPHANIAH (Jehovah/Yahweh is darkness or God hides) **Known Facts** 1. Was the son of Cushi (Zep.1:1). 2. Was a descendant of the righteous King Hezekiah (Zep.1:1). 3. Prophesied to Judah, the Southern Kingdom, helping to lead the way for the religious reforms of Josiah (Zep.1:1). **Predictions and Messages** 1. The prophecy of the coming judgment against Judah and Jerusalem (Zep.1:2-18). 2. The sermon about seeking the LORD to escape His wrath (Zep.2:1-3). 3. The prophecy of the coming judgment against the Philistines (Zep.2:4-7). 4. The prophecy of the coming judgment against Moab and Ammon (Zep.2:8-11). 5. The prophecy of the coming judgment against Cush (Zep.2:12). 6. The prophecy of the coming judgment against Assyria (Zep.2:13-15). 7. The prophecy of the coming judgment against Jerusalem (Zep.3:1-7). 8. The prophecy of the purity of Israel in the last days (Zep.3:8-13; Re.14:1-5). 9. The prophecy of the restoration of Israel and Jerusalem (Zep.3:14-20). **Scripture References** The book of *Zephaniah* (cont. on next page)	**Time** *640-609 B.C., during the entire reign of Josiah, king of Judah, who led the last great revival before the fall of Jerusalem in 586 B.C.* **Place** *Judah, the Southern Kingdom of Israel and Jerusalem, the capital city.*	After Manasseh and Amon, two of the most wicked kings in all of Judah's history, God raised up a godly king—Josiah. It was at the tender age of eight that Josiah was crowned king. Obviously, some consistent and righteous believers had a strong, spiritual influence upon young Josiah, for he lived a righteous life in the sight of the LORD. In fact, Scripture says that he followed the godly example of David, never deviating from the righteous example set by the ancient king (2 K.22:2). During his reign, Josiah had one major concern: the restoration of the temple and the true worship of the LORD, the only living and true God (2 K.22:3-7). No doubt, the prophet Zephaniah was one of the people who had a strong spiritual influence on Josiah. Zephaniah called the people to repent and to turn back to God. They had acted no better than their evil neighbors, and the wrath of God was about to be poured out. But there was still a ray of hope if only the people would repent and change their evil ways. Scripture reveals to us that the nation did listen to Zephaniah and the other prophets of that time and that the invasion of Babylon was delayed because of their change of heart (2 Chr.34:27-28). As a result of the messages of Zephaniah and others, Josiah started one of the two great revivals in Israel's history. (The other was by Hezekiah, the ancestor of Zephaniah.) Zephaniah's message announced the coming terrible judgment of God, in very dark words. But there was also promised blessing and a bright future ahead for those who turned to God. **Gather together, gather together, O shameful nation, before the appointed time arrives and that day sweeps on like chaff, before the fierce anger of the LORD comes upon you, before the day of the LORD's wrath comes upon you. Seek the LORD, all you humble of the land, you who do what he commands. Seek righteousness, seek humility; perhaps you will be sheltered on the day of the LORD's anger (Zep.2:1-3)**	Deep concern for righteousness and for true worship should grip our hearts. For righteousness and true worship determine our destiny, both individually and corporately, as a society and nation. Righteousness builds a character of integrity within people, and righteous individuals build up a nation. If a person is righteous, he is honest, just, true, moral and law-abiding. He keeps the laws of the land and works diligently at his job in order to make a significant contribution to society. Righteousness builds the character of morality and integrity. And when there are enough of us with righteous characters, we build a nation of righteousness, a nation of enormous strength. This can be the experience of any of us. True worship also determines our destiny. If we truly worship the true and living God with a humble and repentant attitude, accepting the sacrifice of His Son, then He will accept us. Think about this glorious truth: The LORD God of the universe, Who sent His Son to die for our sins, is the true and living God who loves us. It is He who is to be worshipped, and He alone. There is a bright future for anyone who turns from sin, lives a righteous life, and truly worships God. **Come back to your senses as you ought, and stop sinning; for there are some who are ignorant of God—I say this to your shame (1 Co.15:34).** **It teaches us to say "No" to ungodliness and worldly passions, and to live self-controlled, upright and godly lives in this present age, while we wait for the blessed hope—the glorious appearing of our great God and Savior, Jesus Christ (Tit.2:12-13).** **Through the blessing of the upright a city is exalted, but by the mouth of the wicked it is destroyed (Pr.11:11).**

PROPHET	TIME/PLACE GIVEN	MAIN MESSAGE	PRACTICAL APPLICATION
ZEPHANIAH (cont.)		"The sorrows for the appointed feasts I will remove from you; they are a burden and a reproach to you. At that time I will deal with all who oppressed you; I will rescue the lame and gather those who have been scattered. I will give them praise and honor in every land where they were put to shame. At that time I will gather you; at that time I will bring you home. I will give you honor and praise among all the peoples of the earth when I restore your fortunes before your very eyes," says the LORD (Zep.3:18-20).	

TIMELINE OF KINGS, PROPHETS AND HISTORY*

HISTORY

DATE BC	FOREIGN KINGS	WORLD EVENTS
1000	Ashur-Rabi II (1010–970) (Assyria) Hiram (1003–966) (Tyre)	David captures Jerusalem (1004)
950	Tiglath-Pileser II (960–935) (Assyria)	Foundation for the Temple (966) 22nd Egyptian Dynasty (945)
930	Shishak I (945–924) (Egypt)	Kingdom Divided (930)
900	Ben-Hadad I (900) (Syria)	Assyria makes peace with Babylon (915)
850	Eth-Baal (887–856) (Sidon) Hazael (840) (Syria)	Jehoshaphat leads a revival (865) Elijah's contest with prophets of Baal (857) Elijah's mantle passed to Elisha (845)
800	Ben-Hadad II (798) (Syria)	Carthage established (814) Joash repairs Temple (812) 23rd Egyptian dynasty (800)
750	Ben-Hadad III (773) (Syria) Rezin (750) (Syria)	Olympic games begin (776) Rome founded (753) Babylonian and Chinese calendar (750)

THE UNITED KINGDOM

BIBLE REF.	KINGS (YEARS REIGNED)	PROPHETS
1 S.16:1-1 K.2:11; 1 Chr.11:1-30	David (40) (1011–971)	Samuel (1095–1015) Gad (1015–950) Asaph (1004)
1 K.2:12-11:43; 1 Chr 28:1-2 Chr.9:31	Solomon (40) (971–931)	Nathan (1003–931) Heman (971)

THE DIVIDED KINGDOM

NORTHERN KINGDOM OF ISRAEL

BIBLE REF.	KINGS (YEARS REIGNED)	PROPHETS
1 K.12:1-24; 12:25-14:20; 2 Chr. 10:1-16	Jeroboam I (22) (931–910)	Ahijah (931–910) Man from Judah (930) Shemaiah (927)
1 K.15:25-31	Nadab (2) (910–909)	
1 K.15:16-16:7; 2 Chr.16:1-6	Baasha (24) (909–886)	Jehu (886)
1 K.16:6-14	Elah (2) (886–885)	
1 K.16:9-20	Zimri (7 days) (885)	Hanani (870)
1 K.16:21-28	Omri (12) (885–874)	
1 K.16:28-22:40; 2 Chr.18:1-34	Ahab (22) (874–853)	Elijah (860–845)
1 K.22:49-51; 2 K. 1:1-18; 2 Chr 20:35-37; 22:1-11	Ahaziah (2) (853–852) Joram/Jehoram (12) (852–841)	Micaiah (853) Elisha (850–795) Eliezer (849–48)
2 K.1:17; 3:1-8:15		
2 K.9:1-10:36; 2 Chr.22:7-9	Jehu (28) (841–814)	
2 K.13:1-9	Jehoahaz (17) (814–798)	
2 K.13:9-25; 14:8-16	Jehoash (16) (798–782)	Zechariah (797)
2 K.14:23-29	Jeroboam II (41) (793–753)	Hosea (788–723) Jonah (780–765)
2 K.15:8-12	Zechariah (6 mos) (753)	Amos (750)
2 K.15:13-15	Shallum (1 mo) (752)	
2 K.15:16-22	Menahem (10) (752–742)	

SOUTHERN KINGDOM OF JUDAH

BIBLE REF.	KINGS (YEARS REIGNED)	PROPHETS
1 K.12:1-24; 14:21-31; 2 Chr.9:31-12:16	Rehoboam (17) (931–913)	Iddo (910) Azariah (896)
1 K.15:1-8; 2 Chr.12:16-14:1	Abijah (3) (913–911)	
1 K.15:9-24; 2 Chr.14:1-16:14	Asa (3) (911–870)	
1 K.22:41-50; 2 K.3:6-14; 2 Chr.17:1-21:1	Jehoshaphat (25) (873–848)	
2 K.8:16-24; 2 Chr.21:1-20	Jehoram (8) (853–841)	Obadiah (845)
2 K.8:25-29; 9:27-29; 2 Chr. 22:1-10	Ahaziah (2) (841)	
2 K.11:1-16; 2 Chr.22:10-23:21	Athaliah (7) (841–835)	Joel (830)
2 K.11:17-12:21; 2 Chr 22:11-12; 24:1-27	Joash/Jehoash (40) (835–796)	
2 K.14:1-20; 2 Chr.24:27-25:28	Amaziah (29) (796–767)	
2 K.14:21-22; 15:1-7; 2 Chr.26:1-23	Azariah/Uzziah (52) (792–740)	Jonah (780–765)
2 K.15:32-38; 2 Chr.26:23-27:9	Jotham (16) (750–731)	

THE DIVIDED KINGDOM

HISTORY

DATE BC	FOREIGN KINGS	WORLD EVENTS
	Tiglath-Pil[n]eser III [or Pul] (745–727) (Assyria)	Assyria takes control of Northern Kingdom (745–627)
	Shalmaneser V (727–722) (Assyria)	Assyria invades Northern Israel (732)
700	So (727–716) (Egypt)	Fall of Northern Kingdom (722)
	Sargon II (710–705) (Assyria)	Sennacherib defeats Egypt (701)
	Sennacherib (705–681) (Assyria)	Hezekiah's tunnel (701)
	Merodach-Baladan (721–710, 705–704) (Assyria)	185,000 Assyrians killed by God (701)
650	Tirhakah (690–664) (Egypt)	Sennacherib destroys Babylon (689)
	Esarhaddon (681–669) (Assyria)	Josiah's reform (621)
	Nabopolassar (626–605) (Assyria)	Nineveh destroyed (612)
	Neco (610–595) (Egypt)	Battle of Carchemish (605)
600	Nebuchadnezzar II (605–562) (Babylon)	1st group of exiles from Judah taken to Babylon (605)
		2nd group of exiles from Judah taken to Babylon (597)
		Fall of Judah—Third group of exiles from Judah taken to Babylon (586)
550	Evil-Merodach (562–560) (Babylon)	Fall of Babylon to Medo-Persian Empire (539)
	Cyrus II (559–530) (Medo-Persia)	Cyrus II decrees that the Jews may return to the Holy Land (538)
	Belshazzar (552–539) (Babylon)	1st exiles return to Holy Land with Zerubbabel (537)
500	Darius I (521–486) (Medo-Persia)	1st Temple foundation laid (536)
		2nd Temple foundation laid (520)
		Temple completed (516)
		Republic of Rome est. (509)
450	Artaxerxes (465–425) (Persia)	2nd return under Ezra (458)
		3rd return under Nehemiah (445)

SOUTHERN KINGDOM OF JUDAH

BIBLE REF.	KINGS (Years Reigned)	PROPHETS
		Isaiah (740–690)
2 K.15:38-16:20; 2 Chr.27:9-27; Is.7:1-9:1	Ahaz (16) (735–715)	Micah (735–725); Oded (733)
2 K.18:1-20:21; 2 Chr.28:27-32:33; Pr.25:1; Is.36:1-39:8	Hezekiah (29) (729–686)	
2 K.20:21-21:18; 2 Chr.32:33-33:20	Manasseh (55) (696–642)	Nahum (663–612)
2 K.21:18-26; 2 Chr.33:20-25	Amon (2) (642–640)	
2 K.21:26-23:30; 2 Chr.33:25-35:27	Josiah (31) (640–609)	Zephaniah (640–609)
2 K.23:31-33; 2 Chr.36:1-4	Jehoaz/Jehoahaz (3 mos) (609)	Jeremiah (627–562)
2 K.23:34-24:7; 2 Chr.36:5-8	Jehoiakim (11) (608–598)	Habakkuk (615–598)
2 K.24:8-17; 25:27-30; 2 Chr.36:8-10;	Jehoiachin (3 mos) (598–597)	Daniel (605–535)
2 K.24:18-25:21; 2 Chr.36:10-14; Je.21:1-52:11	Zedekiah/Mattaniah (11) (597–586)	Ezekiel (593–571)
2 K.25:22-26; Je.40:5-41:18	Gedaliah (2 mos) (Appointed by Nebuchadnezzar) (586)	Haggai (520); Zechariah (520–518)
		Malachi (430)

NORTHERN KINGDOM OF ISRAEL

PROPHETS	KINGS (Years Reigned)	BIBLE REF.
	Pekahiah (2) (742–740)	2 K.15:23-26
	Pekah (20) (752–732) .(752–740) (ruled only in Gilead) (740–732) (ruled in Samaria)	2 K.15:27-31
	Hoshea (9) (732–722)	2 K.17:1-23

The resources used for the Timeline are as follows:

1 The Bible
2 Archer, Gleason L. *Encyclopedia of Bible Difficulties*. (Grand Rapids, Michigan: Zondervan Publishing House), 1982.
3 Freedman, David Noel, ed., et. al. *The Anchor Bible Dictionary*. (New York: Doubleday), 1992.
4 Grun, Bernard. *The Timetables of History*. 3rd ed. (New York: Simon & Schuster), 1991.
5 Kaiser, Walter C. *A History of Israel*. (Nashville, Tennessee: Broadman & Holman Publishers), 1998.
6 Silverman, David P., ed. *Ancient Egypt*. (New York: Oxford University Press), 1997.

ACKNOWLEDGMENTS AND BIBLIOGRAPHY

Every child of God is precious to the LORD and deeply loved. And every child as a servant of the LORD touches the lives of those who come in contact with him or his ministry. The writing ministries of the following servants have touched this work, and we are grateful that God brought their writings our way. We hereby acknowledge their ministry to us, being fully aware that there are so many others down through the years whose writings have touched our lives and who deserve mention, but whose names have faded from our memory. May our wonderful LORD continue to bless the ministries of these dear servants—and the ministries of us all—as we diligently labor to reach the world for Christ and to meet the desperate needs of those who suffer so much.

THE REFERENCE WORKS

Aharoni, Yohanan, Michael Avi-Yonah, Anson F. Rainey and Ze'ev Safrai, Editors. *The MacMillan Bible Atlas*, 3rd Ed. Jerusalem: Carta, The Israel Map and Publishing Company, 1993.

Albright, W.F. *History, Archaeology and Christian Humanism.* New York: McGraw Hill, 1964.

Archer, Gleason L. *A Survey of Old Testament Introduction.* Chicago, IL: Moody Bible Institute of Chicago, 1974.

————. *Encyclopedia of Bible Difficulties.* Grand Rapids, Michigan: Zondervan Publishing House, 1982.

Atlas of the World. Hammond Concise Edition. Maplewood, NJ: Hammond Inc., 1993.

Baker's Dictionary of Theology. Everett F. Harrison, Editor-in-Chief. Grand Rapids, MI: Baker Book House, 1960.

Barker, William P. *Everyone in the Bible.* Westwood, NJ: Fleming H. Revell Co., 1966.

Benware, Paul N. *Survey of the Old Testament.* "Everyman's Bible Commentary." Chicago, IL: Moody Bible Institute of Chicago, 1993.

Bromiley, Geoffrey W., Editor, et. al. *David.* "The International Standard Bible Encyclopedia." Grand Rapids, MI: Eerdmans Publishing Co., 1988.

Brown, Francis. *The New Brown-Driver-Briggs-Gesenius Hebrew-English Lexicon.* Peabody, MA: Hendrickson Publishers, 1979.

Cruden's Complete Concordance of the Old & New Testament. Philadelphia, PA: The John C. Winston Co., 1930.

Dake, Finis Jennings. *Dake's Annotated Reference Bible, The Holy Bible.* Lawrenceville, GA: Dake Bible Sales, Inc., 1963.

Douglas, J.D. Editor. *New Bible Dictionary.* Wheaton, IL: Tyndale House Publishers, Inc., 1982.

Easton's 1897 Bible Dictionary. Database NavPress Software, 1996.

Elwell, Walter A., Editor. *The Evangelical Dictionary of Theology.* Grand Rapids, MI: Baker Book House, 1984.

Enhanced Nave's Topics. Database NavPress Software, 1991, 1994.

Frank, Harry Thomas, ed. *Atlas of the Bible Lands.* Maplewood, NJ: Hammond Incorporated, 1977.

Freedman, David Noel, Editor, et. al. *The Anchor Bible Dictionary.* New York: Doubleday, 1992.

Funk & Wagnalls Standard Desk Dictionary. Lippincott & Crowell, Publishers, 1980, Vol.2.

Geisler, Norman. *A Popular Survey of the Old Testament.* Grand Rapids, MI: Baker Book House, 1977.

Gill, Dr. A.L., Compiler. *God's Promises For Your Every Need.* Dallas, TX: Word Publishing, 1995.

Good News Bible. Old Testament: © American Bible Society, 1976. New Testament: © American Bible Society, 1966, 1971, 1976. Collins World.

Good News for Modern Man, The New Testament. New York, NY: American Bible Society, 1971.

Goodrick, Edward W. and John R. Kohlenberger, III. *The NIV Exhaustive Concordance.* Grand Rapids, MI: Zondervan Publishing House, 1990.

Grun, Bernard. *The Timetables of History.* 3rd Edition. New York: Simon & Schuster, 1991.

Harrison, Roland Kenneth. *Introduction to the Old Testament.* Grand Rapids, MI: Eerdmans Publishing Co., 1969.

Holman Bible Dictionary. Nashville, TN: Broadman & Holman Publishers, 1991. Database NavPress Software.

Hooper, Jerry L., Editor. *The Holman Bible Atlas.* Philadelphia, PA: A.J. Holman Company, 1978.

ISBE. Grand Rapids, MI: Eerdmans Publishing Co., 1988.

Josephus, Flavius. *Complete Works.* Grand Rapids, MI: Kregel Publications, 1981.

Kaiser, Walter C. *A History of Israel.* Nashville, Tennessee: Broadman and Holman Publishers, 1998.

Kipfer, Barbara Ann, Ph.D. *Roget's 21st Century Thesaurus.* New York, NY: Dell Publishing, 1992.

Kohlenberger, John R. III. *The Interlinear NIV Hebrew-English Old Testament.* Grand Rapids, MI: Zondervan Publishing House, 1987.

Kouffman, Donald T. *The Dictionary of Religious Terms.* Westwood, NJ: Fleming H. Revell Co., 1967.

Life Application® Bible. Wheaton, IL: Tyndale House Publishers, Inc., 1991.

Life Application® Study Bible. New International Version. Tyndale House Publishers, Inc.: Wheaton, IL 1991, and Zondervan Publishing House: Grand Rapids, MI, 1984.

Lindsell, Harold and Woodbridge, Charles J. *A Handbook of Christian Truth.* Westwood, NJ: Fleming H. Revell Company, A Division of Baker Book House, 1953.

Living Quotations For Christians. Edited by Sherwood Eliot Wirt and Kersten Beckstrom. New York, NY: Harper & Row, Publishers, 1974.

Lockyer, Herbert. *All the Books and Chapters of the Bible.* Grand Rapids, MI: Zondervan Publishing House, 1966.

————. *All the Kings and Queens of the Bible.* Grand Rapids, MI: Zondervan Publishing House, 1961.

————. *All the Men of the Bible.* Grand Rapids, MI: Zondervan Publishing House, 1958.

————. *All the Miracles of the Bible.* Grand Rapids, MI: Zondervan Publishing House, 1961.

————. *All the Parables of the Bible.* Grand Rapids, MI: Zondervan Publishing House, 1963.

————. *The Women of the Bible.* Grand Rapids, MI: Zondervan Publishing House, 1967.

Luckenbill, Daniel David. *Ancient Records of Assyria and Babylonia,* 2 Vols. (ARAB) London: Histories and Mysteries of Man Ltd., 1989.

Martin, Alfred. *Survey of the Scriptures,* Part I, II, III. Chicago, IL: Moody Bible Institute of Chicago, 1961.

McDowell, Josh. *Evidence That Demands a Verdict,* Vol.1. San Bernardino, CA: Here's Life Publishers, Inc., 1979.

Miller, Madeleine S. & J. Lane. *Harper's Bible Dictionary.* New York, NY: Harper & Row Publishers, 1961.

Nave, Orville J. *Nave's Topical Bible*. Nashville, TN: The Southwestern Company. Copyright © by J.B. Henderson, 1921.

Nelson's Complete Book of Bible Maps & Charts. Nashville, TN: Thomas Nelson Publishers, Inc., 1996.

New American Standard Bible, Updated Edition. La Habra, CA: The Lockman Foundation, 1995.

New Bible Dictionary, 3rd Edition. Leicester, England: Universities & Colleges Christian Fellowship, 1996.

New Living Translation, Holy Bible. Wheaton, IL: Tyndale House Publishers, Inc., 1996.

NIV Thompson Student Bible. Jauchen, John S., Editor, et. al. Indianapolis, IN: Kirkbride Bible Company, 1999.

Orr, James, Editor. *The International Standard Bible Encyclopaedia*, Grand Rapids, MI: Eerdmans Publishing Co., 1939.

Orr, William. *How We May Know That God Is*. Wheaton, IL: Van Kampen Press, n.d.

Owens, John Joseph. *Analytical Key to the Old Testament*, Vols.1, 2, 3. Grand Rapids, MI: Baker Book House, 1989.

Payne, J. Barton. *Encyclopedia of Biblical Prophecy*. New York, NY: Harper & Row, Publishers, 1973.

Pilgrim Edition, Holy Bible. New York, NY: Oxford University Press, 1952.

Ridout, Samuel. *Lectures on the Tabernacle*. New York, NY: Loizeaux Brothers, Inc., 1914.

Silverman, David P. ed. *Ancient Egypt*. New York: Oxford University Press, 1997.

Smith, William. *Smith's Bible Dictionary*. Peabody, MA: Hendrickson Publishers, n.d.

Stone, Nathan J. *Names of God*. Chicago, IL: Moody Press, 1944.

Strong, James. *Strong's Exhaustive Concordance of the Bible*. Nashville, TN: Thomas Nelson, Inc., 1990.

———. *The Tabernacle of Israel*. Grand Rapids, MI: Kregel Publications, 1987.

Strong's Greek and Hebrew Dictionary as compiled by iExalt Software. Database NavPress Software, 1990-1993.

The Amplified Bible. Scripture taken from THE AMPLIFIED BIBLE, Old Testament copyright © 1965, 1987 by the Zondervan Publishing House. The Amplified New Testament copyright © 1958, 1987 by The Lockman Foundation. Used by permission.

The Holy Bible in Four Translations. Minneapolis, MN: Worldwide Publications. Copyright © The Iversen-Norman Associates: New York, NY, 1972.

The Illustrated Bible Atlas, with Historical Notes by F. F. Bruce. Grand Rapids, MI: Kregel Publications, 1994.

The Interlinear Bible, Vols.1, 2, 3. Translated by Jay P. Green, Sr. Grand Rapids, MI: Baker Book House, 1976.

The Interpreter's Bible, 12 Vols. New York, NY: Abingdon Press, 1956.

The NASB Greek/Hebrew Dictionary and Concordance. La Habra, CA: The Lockman Foundation, 1988.

The Nelson Study Bible, New King James Version. Earl D. Radmacher, General Editor. Nashville, TN: Thomas Nelson Publishers, Inc., 1997.

The New Compact Bible Dictionary. Edited by T. Alton Bryant. Grand Rapids, MI: Zondervan Publishing House, 1967. Used by permission of Zondervan Publishing House.

The New Scofield Reference Bible. Edited by C.I. Scofield. New York, NY: Oxford University Press, 1967.

The New Testament-English, PI-RHO. "The Complete Biblical Library." Springfield, MO: World Library Press Inc, 1991.

The New Thompson Chain Reference Bible. Indianapolis, IN: B.B. Kirkbride Bible Co., Inc., 1964.

The New Unger's Bible Dictionary. Chicago, IL: Moody Press, 1998. Database NavPress Software, 1997.

The NIV Study Bible, New International Version. Grand Rapids, MI: Zondervan Publishing House, 1985.

The Old Testament Hebrew-English Dictionary, NUN—AYIN. "The Complete Biblical Library." Springfield, MO: World Library Press Inc., 1999.

The Open Bible. Nashville, TN: Thomas Nelson Publishers, 1977.

The Quest Study Bible. New International Version. Grand Rapids, MI: Zondervan Publishing House, 1994.

The Zondervan Pictorial Encyclopedia of the Bible, Vol.1. Merrill C. Tenney, Editor. Grand Rapids, MI: Zondervan Publishing House, 1982.

Theological Wordbook of the Old Testament. Edited by R. Laird Harris. Chicago, IL: Moody Bible Institute of Chicago, 1980.

Unger, Merrill F. & William White, Jr. *Nelson's Expository Dictionary of the Old Testament*. Nashville, TN: Thomas Nelson Publishers, 1980.

Vine, W.E., Merrill F. Unger, William White, Jr. *Vine's Complete Expository Dictionary of Old and New Testament Words*. Nashville, TN: Thomas Nelson Publishers, 1985.

Walton, John H. *Chronological and Background Charts of the Old Testament*. Grand Rapids, MI: Zondervan Publishing House, 1978.

Webster's Seventh New Collegiate Dictionary. Springfield, MA: G. & C. Merriam Company, Publishers, 1971.

Wilmington. Harold L. *The Outline Bible*. Wheaton, IL: Tyndale House Publishers, Inc., 1999.

Wilson, William. *Wilson's Old Testament Word Studies*. McLean, VA: MacDonald Publishing Company, n.d.

Wood, Leon. *A Survey of Israel's History*. Grand Rapids, MI: Zondervan Publishing House, 1982.

Young, Edward J. *An Introduction to the Old Testament*. Grand Rapids, MI: Eerdmans Publishing Co., 1964.

Young, Robert. *Young's Analytical Concordance to the Bible*. Grand Rapids, MI: Eerdmans Publishing Co., n.d.

Zodhiates, Spiros, Th.D., Executive Editor. *The Hebrew-Greek Key Study Bible, New International Version*. Chattanooga, TN: AMG Publishers, 1996.

Zondervan NIV Bible Library. Version 2.5. Grand Rapids, MI: Zondervan Publishing House.

THE COMMENTARIES

Alexander, Joseph Addison. *The Prophecies of Isaiah*. "The Zondervan Commentary Series." Grand Rapids, MI: Zondervan Publishing House, 1981.

Bultema, Harry. *Isaiah*. Grand Rapids, MI: Kregel Publications, 1981.

Burroughs, P.E., D.D. *Old Testament Studies*. Nashville, TN: Sunday School Board, Southern Baptist Convention, 1915.

Clements, R.E. *Isaiah 1-39*. "The New Century Bible Commentary." Grand Rapids, MI: Eerdmans Publishing Co., 1980.

Criswell, W.A. *Isaiah an exposition*. Grand Rapids, MI: Zondervan Publishing House, 1977.

Elwell, Walter A., Editor. *Topical Analysis of the Bible*. (Grand Rapids, MI: Baker Book House, 1991.

Evans, Mary J. *1 and 2 Samuel*. "New International Biblical Commentary." Peabody, MA: Hendrickson Publishers, Inc., 2000.

Griffin, Gilbert L. *The Gospel in Isaiah*. Nashville, TN: Convention Press, 1968.

Grogan, G.W. *Isaiah*. "The Expositor's Bible Commentary," Vol.6. Grand Rapids, MI: Zondervan Publishing House, 1988.

Henry, Matthew. *Matthew Henry's Commentary*, 6 Vols. Old Tappan, NJ: Fleming H. Revell Co., n.d.

Holladay, William L. *Isaiah: Scroll of a Prophetic Heritage*. Grand Rapids, MI: Eerdmans Publishing Co., 1978.

Horton, Stanley M. *Isaiah*. "The Complete Biblical Library: The Old Testament," Vol.9. Springfield, MO: World Library Press Inc., 1995.

Ironside, H.A. *The Prophet Isaiah*. Neptune, NJ: Loizeaux Brothers, Inc., 1952.

Jennings, F.C. *Studies in Isaiah*. Neptune, NJ: Loizeaux Brothers, Inc., n.d..

Kaiser, Walter C., Jr. *A History of Israel*. Nashville, TN: Broadman & Holman Publishers, 1998.

Keil-Delitzsch. *Commentary on the Old Testament*, Vol.8. Grand Rapids, MI: Eerdmans Publishing Co., n.d.

Kirkpatrick, A.F., General Editor. *The Book of the Prophet Isaiah Chapters I-XXXIX*. "The Cambridge Bible for Schools and Colleges." New York, NY: Cambridge University Press, 1958.

————. *The Book of the Prophet Isaiah Chapters XL-LXVI*. "The Cambridge Bible for Schools and Colleges." New York, NY: Cambridge University Press, 1960.

Leupold, H.C. *Exposition of Isaiah*, Vol.1. Baker Book House, Grand Rapids, Michigan, 1968.

Maclaren, Alexander. *Expositions of Holy Scripture*, 11 Vols. Grand Rapids, MI: Eerdmans Publishing Co., 1952-59.

Martin, Alfred. *Isaiah, The Salvation of Jehovah*. "Everyman's Bible Commentary." Chicago, IL: Moody Bible Institute of Chicago, 1956.

McGee, J. Vernon. *Thru the Bible*, Vol.3. Nashville, TN: Thomas Nelson Publishers, 1982.

McKenna, David. *Isaiah 1-39*. "Mastering the Old Testament," Vol.16A. Dallas, TX: Word Publishing, 1994.

Morgan, G. Campbell. *Living Messages of the Books of the Bible*, Vol.1. Old Tappan, NJ: Fleming H. Revell, 1912.

Morris, Henry M. *The Genesis Record*. Grand Rapids, MI., 1996.

Motyer, J. Alec. *Isaiah* ."The Tyndale Old Testament Commentaries." Downers Grove, IL: Inter-Varsity Press, 1999.

————. *The Prophecy of Isaiah*. Downers Grove, IL: Inter-varsity Press, 1993.

Oswalt, John N. *Isaiah 1-39*. "The New International Commentary on the Old Testament," Grand Rapids, MI: Eerdmans Publishing Co. 1982.

Poole, Matthew. *Matthew Poole's Commentary on the Holy Bible*, Vol.2. Peabody, MA: Hendrickson Publishers, n.d.

Redpath, Alan. *Victorious Christian Service*. Westwood, NJ: Fleming H. Revell Co., 1958.

Schulz, Samuel J. *The Old Testament Speaks*, 4th Edition. San Francisco, CA: Harper Collins Publishers, 1990.

Smith, James E. *What the Bible Teaches about the Promised Messiah*. Nashville, TN: Thomas Nelson Publishers, 1993.

Spurgeon, C.H. *Spurgeon's Sermon Notes. Genesis to Malachi*. Westwood, NJ: Fleming H. Revell Co., n.d.

The Pulpit Commentary. 23 Vols. Edited by H.D.M. Spence & Joseph S. Exell. Grand Rapids, MI: Eerdmans Publishing Co., 1950.

Walvoord, John F. and Roy B. Zuck, Editors. *The Bible Knowledge Commentary, Old Testament*. Colorado Springs, CO: Chariot Victor Publishing, 1985.

Wiersbe, Warren W. *Be Comforted*. Wheaton, IL: Victor Books, 1992.

Willis, John T. *Isaiah*. "The Living Word Commentary on the Old Testament." Abilene, TX: ACU Press, 1984.

Wright, G. Ernest. *Isaiah*. "The Layman's Bible Commentary," Vol.11. Atlanta, GA: John Knox Press, 1964.

Young, Edward J. *The Book of Isaiah*, Vol.1. Grand Rapids, MI: Eerdmans Publishing Co., 1965

OUTLINE BIBLE RESOURCES

This material, like similar works, has come from imperfect man and is thus susceptible to human error. We are nevertheless grateful to God for both calling us and empowering us through His Holy Spirit to undertake this task. Because of His goodness and grace, *The Preacher's Outline & Sermon Bible*® New Testament and Old Testament volumes are now complete.

The Minister's Personal Handbook, The Believer's Personal Handbook, and other helpful **Outline Bible Resources** are available in printed form as well as releasing electronically on various software programs.

God has given the strength and stamina to bring us this far. Our confidence is that as we keep our eyes on Him and remain grounded in the undeniable truths of the Word, we will continue to produce other helpful Outline Bible Resources for God's dear servants to use in their Bible Study and discipleship.

We offer this material, first, to Him in whose Name we labor and serve and for whose glory it has been produced, and, second, to everyone everywhere who preaches and teaches the Word.

Our daily prayer is that each volume will lead thousands, millions, yes, even billions, into a better understanding of the Holy Scriptures and a fuller knowledge of Jesus Christ the Incarnate Word, of whom the Scriptures so faithfully testify.

You will be pleased to know that Leadership Ministries Worldwide partners with Christian organizations, printers, and mission groups around the world to make Outline Bible Resources available and affordable in many countries and foreign languages. It is our goal that *every* leader around the world, both clergy and lay, will be able to understand God's Holy Word and to present God's message with more clarity, authority, and understanding— all beyond his or her own power.

LEADERSHIP MINISTRIES WORLDWIDE
PO Box 21310 • Chattanooga, TN 37424-0310
(423) 855-2181 • FAX (423) 855-8616
info@lmw.org
www.lmw.org - FREE Download materials

LEADERSHIP MINISTRIES WORLDWIDE

Publishers of Outline Bible Resources

- **THE PREACHER'S OUTLINE & SERMON BIBLE®** (POSB) • **KJV – NIV**

NEW TESTAMENT

Matthew 1 (chapters 1–15)
Matthew 2 (chapters 16–28)
Mark
Luke
John
Acts
Romans

1 & 2 Corinthians
Galatians, Ephesians, Philippians, Colossians
1 & 2 Thessalonians, 1 & 2 Timothy, Titus, Philemon
Hebrews, James
1 & 2 Peter, 1, 2, & 3 John, Jude
Revelation
Master Outline & Subject Index

OLD TESTAMENT

Genesis 1 (chapters 1–11)
Genesis 2 (chapters 12–50)
Exodus 1 (chapters 1–18)
Exodus 2 (chapters 19–40)
Leviticus
Numbers
Deuteronomy
Joshua
Judges, Ruth
1 Samuel
2 Samuel

1 Kings
2 Kings
1 Chronicles
2 Chronicles
Ezra, Nehemiah, Esther, Job
Psalms 1 (chapters 1-41)
Psalms 2 (chapters 42-106)
Psalms 3 (chapters 107-150)
Proverbs
Ecclesiastes, Song of Solomon

Isaiah 1 (chapters 1-35)
Isaiah 2 (chapters 36-66)
Jeremiah 1 (chapters 1-29)
Jeremiah 2 (chapters 30-52),
   Lamentations
Ezekiel
Daniel, Hosea
Joel, Amos, Obadiah, Jonah,
   Micah, Nahum
Habakkuk, Zephaniah, Haggai,
   Zechariah, Malachi

Print versions of all Outline Bible Resources are available in various forms.

- *What the Bible Says to the Believer* — **The Believer's Personal Handbook**
  11 Chs. – Over 500 Subjects, 300 Promises, & 400 Verses Expounded - Italian Imitation Leather or Paperback

- *What the Bible Says to the Minister* — **The Minister's Personal Handbook**
  12 Chs. - 127 Subjects - 400 Verses Expounded - Italian Imitation Leather or Paperback

- **Practical Word Studies In the New Testament** — 2 Vol. Hardcover Set

- **The Teacher's Outline & Study Bible™ - Various New Testament Books**
  Complete 30 - 45 minute lessons – with illustrations and discussion questions

- **Practical Illustrations — Companion to the POSB**
  Arranged by topic and Scripture reference

- **What the Bible Says About Series – Various Subjects**

- **OBR on various digital platforms**
  See current digital providers on our website at www.lmw.org

- **Translations of various books**
  See our website for more information or contact our office

— Contact LMW for quantity orders and information —

LEADERSHIP MINISTRIES WORLDWIDE or Your Local Christian Bookstore
PO Box 21310 • Chattanooga, TN 37424-0310
(423) 855-2181 • FAX (423) 855-8616 (Mon. - Thurs. 9am – 5pm Eastern)
E-mail - info@lmw.org • Order online at www.lmw.org

PURPOSE STATEMENT

LEADERSHIP MINISTRIES WORLDWIDE

exists to equip ministers, teachers, and laymen in their understanding, preaching, and teaching of God's Word by publishing and distributing worldwide *The Preacher's Outline & Sermon Bible®* and related **Outline Bible Resources**; to reach & disciple men, women, boys and girls for Jesus Christ.

MISSION STATEMENT

1. To make the Bible so understandable – its truth so clear and plain – that men and women everywhere, whether teacher or student, preacher or hearer, can grasp its message and receive Jesus Christ as Savior, and...

2. To place the Bible in the hands of all who will preach and teach God's Holy Word, verse by verse, precept by precept, regardless of the individual's ability to purchase it.

The **Outline Bible Resources** have been given to LMW for printing and especially distribution worldwide at/below cost, by those who remain anonymous. One fact, however, is as true today as it was in the time of Christ:

THE GOSPEL IS FREE, BUT THE COST OF TAKING IT IS NOT

LMW depends on the generous gifts of believers with a heart for Him and a love for the lost. They help pay for the printing, translating, and distributing of **Outline Bible Resources** into the hands of God's servants worldwide, who will present the Gospel message with clarity, authority, and understanding beyond their own.

LMW was incorporated in the state of Tennessee in July 1992 and received IRS 501 (c)(3) nonprofit status in March 1994. LMW is an international, nondenominational mission organization. All proceeds from USA sales, along with donations from donor partners, go directly to underwrite our translation and distribution projects of **Outline Bible Resources** to preachers, church and lay leaders, and Bible students around the world.

www.ingramcontent.com/pod-product-compliance
Lightning Source LLC
Chambersburg PA
CBHW081258040426

42452CB00014B/2562